Wrestling for Blessing

Wrestling for Blessing

MARILYN MCCORD ADAMS

First published in 2005 by
Darton, Longman and Todd Ltd
1 Spencer Court
140–142 Wandsworth High Street
London SW18 4JJ

ISBN 0–232–52584–6

Designed by Sandie Boccacci
Phototypeset in 11.5/15pt Galliard
by Intype Libra Ltd
Printed and bound in Great Britain by
Page Bros, Norwich, Norfolk

CONTENTS

Contents

PART THREE
Whose Purity?

INTRODUCTION

The same night [Jacob] arose and took his two wives, his two maids, and his eleven children, and crossed the ford of Jabbok. He took them and sent them across the stream, and likewise everything that he had. And Jacob was left alone; and a man wrestled with him until the breaking of the day. When the man saw that he did not prevail against Jacob, he touched the hollow of his thigh; and Jacob's thigh was put out of joint as he wrestled with him. Then he said, 'Let me go, for the day is breaking.' But Jacob said, 'I will not let you go, unless you bless me.' And he said to him, 'What is your name?' And he said, 'Jacob.' Then he said, 'Your name shall no more be called Jacob but Israel, for you have striven with God and with men, and have prevailed.' Then Jacob asked him, 'Tell me, I pray, your name.' But he said, 'Why is it that you ask my name?' And there he blessed him. So Jacob called the name of the place Peniel, saying 'For I have seen God face to face, and yet my life is preserved.' The sun rose upon him as he passed Penuel, limping because of his thigh. (Genesis 32:22–31)

Problematic Goodness, Damaging Church

These sermons were preached for those who find God's Goodness problematic. Many were people of considerable (if sometimes unconventional) spiritual experience, people who had at many and various times in their lives tasted and seen God's Goodness – in sunbeam, leaf or flower; in the joy of running, in the wonder and surprises of child-rearing, in the thrill of making glorious music, in the contemplative concentration of intellectual work, in the theatrical intensity of making dramatic roles come alive. Many had at one time or another warmed to the kiss of Divine love, in the care of grandparents and teachers, friends and lovers. Most had felt the confronting, undergirding, all-encompassing Presence, in morning worship or private Bible study, in green cathedrals and awesome mountain tops, in meditation exercises or group prayer.

Yet, they were also people whose suffering penetrates their souls so deeply, whose participation in public and private horrors so stains their lives as to become the demon they must wrestle at the margins for the dawn of blessing. Many had been abused repeatedly – emotionally, physically and sexually – by parents and teachers; by partners and work-supervisors. Some were gay, lesbian or bisexual; others were straight. Some were Vietnam veterans. Others were survivors of violent homes, even of life on the streets. Still others had joined the battle for their sanity against bizarre brain chemistry or for their lives in the war against AIDS. These congregations cut a swatch through racial and class lines. Most people had finished high school. Many had attended some college, even earned professional diplomas. Almost all held advanced degrees in the school of hard knocks.

When terrible things happened to them, they cried to God in their troubles. The results were confusing. Their experience of God's Goodness had led them to expect the Good Shepherd to leave the ninety-nine, to come to their rescue. Sue, an outwardly well-off white woman with evangelical roots, remembered: 'Every night I prayed that Jesus would send guardian angels. Instead someone else . . . my father . . . entered my bedroom, my bed, my body, every night. At first I asked what I was doing wrong. Why was Jesus abandoning me, when I was trying so hard to be a good girl?' Dennis, an African-American of Pentecostal background, prayed every week that his father wouldn't come home. But almost every week he did, hauled the little boy to the outhouse and beat him within an inch of his life. Where was the heavenly Father who poured down Holy Spirit, energising ecstatic dancing and clapping, adorning heads with tongues of flame? Where was God now that he really needed him? Their experience of human evil contradicted their picture of Divine protection, their childlike expectation of tender loving care. Was God really mean and capricious? Harsh and demanding, ready to destroy you for the slightest infraction? Only interested so long as you filled the belly of Divine need? Or (and was or wasn't this worse yet?) didn't God really care?

For many, the Church had turned in a poor performance. Having first come to the knowledge and love of God in the Church, they turned to the

Christian community for help with discernment. Often they were greeted with uncomprehending condemnation, stunned as an iron curtain crashed down to screen them out. Certainly in the 1950s, but even in the 1960s and 1970s, there was at best a conspiracy of silence, at worst a blame-the-victim posture towards spousal and child abuse. For how long did the Church mirror the wider society in enforcing a 'don't ask/don't tell' policy about homosexual orientation? Ted's childhood home was broken and chaotic. His mother was a prostitute who eventually died of syphilis. His father was a drug pusher, who also stole vehicles and charged large fees to smuggle illegal immigrants across the border in the trunks of cars. But Ted was 'saved' when a charismatic congregation took him in, enlisted him in neighbourhood youth activities. Ted learned discipline, began to study not only the Bible, but the three Rs in school. By his mid-teens, he was the local success story; everyone found him extremely bright and promising. One night during a revival meeting, Ted had a dramatic religious experience: flooded with light and filled with the Holy Spirit, he felt called into the Christian ministry. About the same time another fact began to dawn on him. When Ted shared with his religious mentors that he was gay, they immediately denounced him as an 'abomination to the Lord' and assured him that he would go straight to hell if he didn't change his orientation. For Ted, as for many in the congregations I served, the Church had shoved Jesus off the judgement seat, claimed Divine authority to excommunicate, and proceeded to 'cast into outer darkness where there is weeping and gnashing of teeth'. The Church wove, rehung a thick veil of respectability, walling off the Holy of Holies: street and family violence, substance-abusers and -profiteers, crippling mental illness, sexual irregularities, white-collar embezzlers and gangland theft become invisible, simply do not exist in the household of God!

A few – like Ted – were literally cast out. Many others were taught to compartmentalise. The Church was prepared to accept them conditionally, provided they donned the wedding garment of a respectable persona. The god thus advertised was cut down to size. Instead of the sea-parting, grave-bursting God of the Bible, the Church offered a deity who shares the need of human authority figures to believe they are doing a good job, the blindness of human institutions to how bad things really are, and their refusal to recognise what they don't know how to fix. Public worship was a place for pardoning peccadillos, offering and accepting polite apologies, above all for pretending that everything was already all right. Sunday services were scenes where failure and loss were scarcely acknowledged, and even death was advertised as a blessing. The message was strong and effective: people with real problems should take them elsewhere; they should definitely not disturb the peace of 'organised religion' and its conventional god.

People are resourceful, gifted with imagination, with memory, reason and skill. Left to their own devices, members of my congregations – like Jacob – had met their crises with ingenuity. Some threw themselves into developing their talents. With workaholic frenzy, they piled up achievements in business or law, acting or design, dancing or academe. Others dared to colour outside the lines, to chart new paths, by trial and error to invent new lifestyles. Many signed on for long courses of therapy – Freudian, Jungian, Gestalt, eclectic; others embraced self-improvement programmes. Significant numbers tried other religions: 'New Age' mixtures, scientology, native American spirituality, westernised versions of Sufism, Hinduism and Zen. Most had mixed strategies, whose combined effect had been to open personal space to grow and explore, to discover and develop in significant ways.

Yet for many, the spiritual wounds were so deep, the pain so great as eventually to drown their solutions. Some had breakdowns; some turned to alcohol or other drugs; still others got sucked into a downward spiral of destructive relationships; careers crashed; marriages broke; a few even fell into lives of crime. Others tried, yes, succeeded in being good and faithful. But AIDS was gobbling up friends, colleagues, acquaintances, devouring their whole social network at an alarming rate. Looking Death in the face week after week, month upon month leaves a vacuum in the soul.

Church-damaged and battered by life, 'bottomed out' yet rich in experience, these people followed labyrinthian paths to the sanctuary door, and tip-toed back to church. For Ted and others, Alcoholics Anonymous and other 12-step programmes had turned their lives around and laid a groundwork for stability. Many remembered stories of a God who was bigger than Death. Somehow in their rough and tumble, they had bumped into a sense of the Presence, recognisable but long lost. They came eager for good news, in search of a spiritually coherent interpretation of their lives. Because their formation had been Christian, they were giving the Church another chance, wondering whether she could be different and whether the Bible really condemned them, devoutly hoping that the Gospel could be proclaimed in a different key.

World-Smashing Data, Honest Polarities

Developmental psychologists like to imagine that human beings are from the beginning like scientists: bombarded with stimuli from the outside, the organism tries with all its might to impose some stable order on the data of its experience. At first, the infant cannot succeed at all. Then at around three months, the child is able to imprint on, centre its subjective world around, the presence of the mother's face. This world goes-to-smash several months later when the child gets smarter and comes to recognise the absence of the face. As theorisers, we always oversimplify, marginalising some of our data. Human development charts a spiral in which – due to the individual's growing cognitive and affective capacities and the expanding wealth of acknowledged inputs – world orders collapse as overlooked data become salient, demand richer schemes that can handle greater complexity with increased unity. Once achieved, the new world order is inhabited for a while, as the agent gathers strength to confront further challenges.

Human cosmos-creating capacities are geared to things here below, to rocks and trees, mountains and rivers, earth and sky, dogs and cats, other human beings. We are built to enjoy chocolate and Mozart, Alpine scenery, Rembrandt and Picasso, tennis and chess, building a business, understanding physics and making historical discoveries, falling in love, or the birth of a child. Our considerable problem-solving capacities are geared to small, medium, even large-sized obstacles: how to lift stones to build pyramids; how to replace hips and heart valves and to develop vaccines for the latest infectious disease; how to find or retool for a new job; sometimes to recover from rejection and loss, get a fresh start on personal relationships.

Both immense good and horrendous evils are difficult to domesticate; they seem always to crash in, to shatter. The Bible tells us how when God comes down from heaven the earth quakes, volcanoes erupt, belch fire and smoke, mountains and hills skip like rams, waters part, river beds are bared, oak trees writhe. 'Tremble, O earth, at the presence of the Lord, at the presence of the God of Jacob.' Mountains and hills, rivers and oaks are creature-sized furnishings, by nature unsuited for giants or gods. When Divine Presence breaks through the natural order with miracles, or greets people along their paths, they are amazed, fall on their faces with fear. 'Depart from me, for I am a sinful man, O Lord.' Likewise, horrendous evils so eat away the centre of life's positive meaning as to make us wonder whether life can ever again be worth living, whether it would not have been better never to have been born.

Vivid experience of unfathomable good and intimate acquaintance with horrors each create a crisis: how can we organise our world, make it comprehensible, and yet fit either in? The difficulty rises exponentially when – like many in my congregations, college-town as well as urban – a person encounters first one and then the other, or both together, repeatedly. What sense can life make to us, if it includes Goodness without measure *and* evil ghastly beyond words? With experience so polarised, sanity virtually requires us to repress the one and underestimate the other. Because each datum is so intense, in its own way so convincing, such solutions are unstable. What is pushed down demands to come up, teeter-totter fashion, each extreme taking its turn to distort our world-view.

For members of my congregations, such dialectics responded to the (often underground) query, which experience represents the face of the real God? The Bible is full of images and models. Polarised experience rips them out of context, isolates them from each other, producing one-dimensional caricatures of the Divine. Subtlety comes in the way one is allowed to colour, nuance the other. 'Who is Jesus?' the synoptic gospels ask. Davidic Messiah, riding into the royal city to take command? Apocalyptic Son of Man descending on the clouds with angelic legions, announcing the great and terrible Day of the Lord? The suffering servant of YHWH? 'All of the above.' Take the first without the third, and you echo Satan's temptation and repeat Peter's mistake at Caesarea Philippi. Seize the second without the first and third, and you make Divine redemption otherworldly, make unintelligible how the Crucified could fill this role. To identify Jesus with all of them requires ironic reversal, and we must wrestle Scripture for the details.

Again, most models are many-sided; they can be taken in a variety of different ways. If we are sure of condemnation and torment, Divine judgement is bad news. But legal imagery can capture inescapable Divine good-pleasure; the notions of verdict and acquittal can express the finality with which God's saying so makes us 'right with God'. For Sue, 'Heavenly Father' would conjure the nightly rapist; for Dennis, a cruel tyrant; for Ted, an unscrupulous crook. Yet for others it symbolises disciplined nurture, wisdom and providential care. Is Jesus really a *good* shepherd of his flock? Or does cross-bearing discipleship show that – like Moloch – he means to devour the lambs?

Incidentally, this is what makes the challenge to use more 'inclusive' language for God both urgent and difficult to meet. In attempting to understand who God is and how God loves, we cannot help reaching for analogies in human social roles. Abstract or ad hoc categories (such as 'First Cause' or 'Heavenly Parent') cannot bear the weight of the richest personal relationships in the cosmos. We need images that root down into the core of our being and network out through the fabric of our experience. But this very depth guarantees that all such models – 'Father', 'Mother', 'Brother', 'Sister', 'Lover', 'Friend', 'Teacher', 'Healer', 'Lover' – will be multiply loaded for good and ill, with experiences of abuse as well as nurture, of repressive control as well as structured empowerment, of devouring demand as well as enabling companionship. Once again, the key to transformation lies in how the images interpret one another. Thus, except where homogeneous special interests gather, communal worship is probably better served by experimental juxta-position of a variety of images than by a mechanical search-and-replace of 'Father' with 'Mother' or 'Father-Mother', any one of which by itself could fall flat for everybody or trample someone else's toes!

Aids to Integration

For those who have drunk deeply of both good and evil, God splits into multiple personalities, who fight with each other, perpetuating conflict at the un-conscious level. Salvation means peace and harmony, which bring integrity to the equally fragmented self. Happily, the Holy Spirit, who moved over chaos at the dawn of creation, labours to give birth to integrity within each and every person. If the Holy Spirit were not intimately present to each of us, we could not be spiritual beings, but at most animals with fancier computers than the apes. Like the mother's face in rela-tion to her infant, the Holy Spirit broods over us evok-ing our potentiality to be spirit, drawing us out before we have any consciousness of self or other, whether or not we can recognise, articulate what is going on. St Paul says, the Spirit groans within us with sighs too deep for words, and we respond with babbling even unconscious acquaintance. Like mother-love, the Spirit's presence strengthens, empowers us to grow and learn. Our Paraclete and inner teacher, the self-effacing Spirit, is ever the midwife of creative insight, subtly nudging, suggesting, directing our attention until we leap to the discovery that '2 + 2 = 5'. Human nature is not created to function independently, but in omnipresent partnership with its Maker. In that wider life where things are clearer, God more obvious, ante-mortem atheists and agnostics will have a chuckle over this silent collaboration, have to acknowledge that the joke is on them!

Mother Church, the family she gathers, should nurture us. She should show us how to bring this indwelling Presence up to consciousness and help us to articulate what the Spirit teaches as well as who the Spirit is. If everyone receives the Spirit, if everyone grows and flourishes in collaboration with it, still – as with parent–child interactions – certain dimensions of the relationship cannot develop without mutual acknowledgement, recognition, conscious, intentional give and take. Because of the 'size gap', figuring out who God is, what God purposes, is a task beyond the competence of any individual or generation. But the Spirit has been with us from the dawn of creation, not only revealing God's own Self to us, but opening our eyes to see, our ears to hear, our mouths to speak.

Within the Church, the Bible is a principal tool of spiritual formation. For Christians, searching holy Scriptures is a skilful means for getting to know who God really is and, at the same time, for discovering our own true selves. They are the texts from which we begin and to which we daily return in trying to understand what is going on in our traffic with God. Usually, the stories come first: we hear, read them over and over, get drawn into their suspense, learn to detect their irony, guffaw at their slapstick humour until they stuff our imaginations and remodel us in their likeness. Becoming vulnerable to the Bible, we give the Spirit permission to make its plots and characters interpretive keys to narrative movements in our own lives. We are Abram, called to leave home and to embrace unknown Divine destiny. We are Trickster Jacob, wrestling for stolen blessing, limping triumphant, marked by God! We are Naomi and Ruth, impoverished but resourceful, learning how two are better than one. We are Isaiah who sees the Lord and volunteers; Jeremiah who feels that God has seduced him. We are Mother Mary perplexed by her Son's strange lifestyle; angry Martha in the kitchen; weeping Magdalene at the tomb.

Curious Christians will experience the lure of making God's more intimate acquaintance and so be drawn to daily study of holy Scriptures. They will be willing to break open the text from many angles and eagerly welcome a variety of interpretive tools for whatever harvest they may yield. Those who have both tasted Divine Goodness and drained the cup of spiced and foaming wine will not be able to approach the Bible passively, as if it were an answer-book to be swallowed whole like some giant doctrinal pill. For them – for how many of us? – the path to integrity lies in setting their polarised experiences, their Jekyl–Hyde portraits of God up against the texts of holy Scriptures. Their way forward lies in imitating rabbis and medieval schoolmen who make holy Scriptures the pre-text and medium of their questioning and disputing with God. 'Did you really command genocide for the Canaanite cities?' 'Why didn't you let Moses enter the promised land after all that work?' 'Are you still against the remarriage of divorced persons?' 'Who are we, that you should take flesh and tabernacle with us?' 'Why do you step in only *after* the worst has already happened?' 'Do you really hate the work of your hands enough to condemn us to the fires of hell as punishment for what we do in this life?'

Liturgy, community worship, also helps to pull us into focus; for liturgies are identity-conferring dramas. Christian rites enact a historic communal sense of who we are individually and collectively in relation to God, one another and the world. Over the centuries, Christians have evolved a rich diversity of styles of common worship, reflecting distinctive insights and sensibilities. This is natural and healthy, because people are different, become open to Divine Presence and to others in different ways.

In this connection, it did not surprise me that our 'medium high' Anglican liturgy, with its eucharistic centre, its variety of postures and wealth of props, especially appealed to the people in my congregations. Most obviously, many were searching for ways to take steps in God's direction, even though their thoughts were confused and their feelings conflicted. They were intimidated by services that 'front-and-centred' intellectual content. They were scared away by styles of worship that emphasised 'correct' belief or the unequivocal commitment of the conscious self. What these people were ready to do was to put their bodies in the pew, kneeling and standing, bowing and crossing themselves; to shape their mouths around the scripted words, tighten and loosen their vocal chords to hymns and chant; to open themselves to incense and holy water, changing colours, smells and bells – all to see if they could stumble into a favourable connection with God. Many who came were spiritually stuck and didn't know how to proceed. Our rituals bombarded them with symbols that could set off unconscious chain reactions and release trapped spiritual energy without their having to know how it worked.

Specifically, holy Eucharist drew them in because of its power to focus both their problem and its solution. By Christ's own institution, holy Eucharist is the way we re-present, show forth, the Lord's death. With sighs too deep for words, they recognised there the horrendous caricatures they felt they were, could face what they had become through the violence of others and by their own hands. There eventually they could rage and cry, 'What kind of God are you who makes the innocent suffer for the guilty? Who abandons us to our own devices and despair?' Holy Eucharist also proclaims God as the One who takes on our caricature, cancels abandonment, according to Anglican understanding becomes really present *here and now* under forms of bread and wine. Eating and drinking signals transformation, makes us members of Christ's Body, already participants in his resurrection life.

Of course, for those who have known and been known by both horrendous evil and the Goodness of God, the very richness of Scriptures and liturgy can also give rise to confusion. Here preaching can help by offering explicit interpretations and by problematising them in an articulate way. My hope in these sermons was and is to foster reintegration by proclaiming the good news of God's Love in a different tone of voice, specifically by sounding three recurrent themes. *The*

21

first is an appreciation of the 'size-gap' between God and creatures. Christian commitment to a personal God is fundamental. Yet, human psychodynamics and political rhetoric easily distort it, representing God as a Jack-and-the-beanstalk giant, only an order-of-magnitude bigger than parents or teachers or monarchs like King Henry VIII; framing Divine–human relations with legal models emphasising obligations and punishments. These sermons counter that God is infinite and eternal; the whole cosmos – much less human beings – finite and temporary, in relation to God a tiny speck. God is much too big to be an authority figure and we are much too small to be adolescent children or adult citizens; the size-gap is too great for rights and obligations to be the principal issue between us. Rather God is in the business of rearing infants; God is resourceful in setting things right, in healing and teaching us how to bear his family resemblance, relentlessly working to draw us up into full stature.

The second is that God can turn anything to blessing because God is Emmanuel, God-with-us, in Christ crucified identifying with the worst that we can suffer, be or do. Because God is not aloof, our wounds and stains become holy ground. God is unveiled as the right One to wrestle for the blessing, because to struggle with God is already in a way to be blessed.

The third (noted above) *recommends utter candour as a strategy for wrestling.* Love is God's nature; blessing was God's purpose in creation. Vivid experience of suffering and evil shouts that the opposite must be so. The suffering and the compromised will not be able to believe that blessing is theirs without imitating Job, dropping the masks of liturgical politeness, with all the pain and fear and rage 'telling it like it is', confronting God with how bad it seems from our human point of view. My effort in these sermons was to practise what I preach: to bring the deep experience of God's omnipresent Goodness up against the nitty-gritty worst that life offers, to do it repeatedly so that we might eventually recognise God as really present in the horrors and thereby experience how the highest joys and the deepest terror, the brightest blessing and the darkest curse find their integration in the heart of God!

For me, the perspective of these sermons was first evoked in the context of urban congregations in the throes of multiple corporate and public emergencies – e.g., the AIDS epidemic, rising homelessness partly due to government funding cuts and the closing of mental hospitals, and multi-ethnic tensions culminating in riots. When I moved from Los Angeles to an East Coast college town, from a large secular university to a divinity school, I discovered that polarised experience of the best good and the worst evils was not geographically isolated, but only differently disguised. Private horrors recur and fester among conventionally respectable people in what passes for ordinary time. I have learned by watching God at work in each of the congregations I served – in the Episcopal Diocese of Los Angeles, Trinity Church, Hollywood; St Augustine's-by-the-Sea, Santa Monica; and St Mary's, Palms; in the Episcopal Diocese of Connecticut, Christ Church, New Haven and St Thomas', New Haven – and I am grateful to each for the privilege of being among them. In these sermons, I offer the blessings for which we wrestled, with the hope that they may furnish others with fresh clues!

MARILYN MCCORD ADAMS
Christ Church, Oxford

PART ONE

'Show us who God is!'

ONE

'Show us who God is, and we shall be satisfied!'

'Do not let your hearts be troubled. Believe in God, believe also in me. In my Father's house there are many dwelling places. If it were not so, would I have told you that I go to prepare a place for you? And if I go and prepare a place for you, I will come again and will take you to myself, so that where I am, there you may be also. And you know the way to the place where I am going.' Thomas said to him, 'Lord, we do not know where you are going. How can we know the way?' Jesus said to him, 'I am the way, and the truth, and the life. No one comes to the Father except through me. If you know me, you will know my Father also. From now on you do know him and have seen him.'

Philip said to him, 'Lord, show us the Father, and we will be satisfied.' Jesus said to him, 'Have I been with you all this time, Philip, and you still do not know me? Whoever has seen me has seen the Father. How can you say, "Show us the Father"? Do you not believe that I am in the

*Father and the Father is in me? The words that I say to
you I do not speak on my own; but the Father who dwells
in me does his works. Believe me that I am in the Father
and the Father is in me; but if you do not, then believe me
because of the works themselves. Very truly, I tell you, the
one who believes in me will also do the works that I do
and, in fact, will do greater works than these, because I
am going to the Father. I will do whatever you ask in my
name, so that the Father may be glorified in the Son. If in
my name you ask me for anything, I will do it.'*

(John 14:1–14)

Most people are aware at one time or another of a deep
desire to give and receive love, to know and be known
and fully accepted, just as we are. We read in books,
and some of us believe in our heads, that God is the
answer to these desires.

But who is God? When we meet someone more
'into' religion than we are, who has obviously spent
more time in prayer, or radiates a kind of holiness, we
hope that they will know. In one way and another, we
beg, 'Show us who God is, and we shall be satisfied.'
We read the Bible, participate in liturgy, say our prayers
with the same background question: Who is God? And
what and how do we have to do with each other?

Of course, some answers are presupposed in the
prayers we have already learned to say.

At least every Sunday, we recite, 'Our Father in
heaven . . .'. What feelings does that bring up in you?
A sense of warm, secure, strong provision? Of
inexhaustible know-how and patient willingness to

teach? Or is it rather a stiff formality of children who are to be seen and not heard? When you pray 'your will be done', is it with a child's happy confidence in the parent full of wonderful surprises? Or do you think of Jesus in the Garden the night before his passion, harbour dark suspicions that the Father's expectations will be harsh, alien, dangerous to your health? Or do you seek the Father's will with the hope that if you are very, very good maybe he will love you after all? Or is your formal tone a signal that God had better keep his distance? Do you secretly fear that his intimacy will not respect your boundaries, that God will overwhelm, wipe you out personally, the way others in your life have tried to do?

Some prayers address our Lord and Saviour Jesus Christ. Does he perhaps feel safer, friendlier than the Father? Do you imagine yourselves as one of those little children who were blessed when they crawled up into his lap? Does he put his arm around you when it hurts the most, and say, 'There, there'. Or is Jesus older brother, running with you, teaching you how to run, how to pray, how to love? Is Jesus your example of loyalty and courage? Is he your mentor? Do you long to imitate him in all things?

Most of us come to church because deep down 'we would see' God 'in Jesus'. Most of us do, at least through a glass darkly, and what we glimpse makes us long for more. But today, as in Bible times, not everybody can. Some shy away, steer clear of Jesus, because they see him as a powerless fellow victim of an aloof or tyrannical God, his cross the unbearable reminder of our fate in a hostile world. Others see the prototype male saviour, who first strips women of their power and self-esteem, coerces us into dependence, then demands eternal subservience in return for the rescue he provides. One young woman explained recently, 'They taught me in church I had to be grateful to Jesus because he died for my sins. But why should I? I didn't ask him to do it! No one consulted me!'

Our Scriptures hint at it only occasionally, but have you ever tried praying to Mommy? Would that make it easier to be vulnerable, to be with God in your failures? Would it make you more confident of God's comfort and willing help? Or do you shudder at the thought of omniscient manipulation, designing inescapable guilt trips and no-win double binds, of omnipotent smother-love that won't let her little darling grow up, be independent, have a mind or will of your own?

What would it be like to address 'Our Goddess'? Did that make your defences shoot up like the Berlin wall? Was it because the very word 'goddess' has connotations of the erotic . . . because attributing sexuality to God violates some dark taboo? Besides, we are enlightened enough to *know* that God is spirit and therefore has no body or sexuality; right? Or does the suggestion give you goose bumps of anticipation, like one woman I knew, who said, 'My whole (fundamentalist) upbringing taught me to feel guilty about being a forceful person. But if it is the Goddess who is omnipotent, then my power is in her image and makes me good!'

When it comes to relating to God, we find ourselves in a predicament! Because God is so big and we are so small, we have no choice but to begin with analogies.

Because God is personal, we appeal to models of human relationships. The trouble is that all of these images are many sided, each coloured by our life experience, evoke various combinations of good and bad. Without really thinking about it, we project both sides of the ambivalence onto the heavens, make God in their image and play out our role accordingly. No wonder our relationships with God can be so confining and confusing! Yet, how do we get out of this maze?

The first thing to do is try to relax. God isn't up tight about the names and titles we use. God knows who God is; the blessed Trinity are secure in their identities. They also know who we are, about the limitations of our factory equipment, and the distortions our experience brings. If you've stopped praying, really, except for the prayers you read out of books in church, the Good News is that God is eager to renew the conversation under whatever image will make you feel most comfortable. After all, as people get to know each other better, there is a continual process of revising who each thinks the other is. So it doesn't matter very much where you begin.

A second corollary of Divine flexibility is that – more than the best of therapists – God is so trustworthy, God's acceptance so unconditional, that we can safely talk openly about our difficulties relating to God with the blessed Trinity themselves. If applying certain images to God makes you cringe or wince or worse, tell God about it. To be sure, some models are more appropriate than others. But strong visceral reactions are usually rooted in the traumas of our past experience. Saying to God, 'You know, it really freaks me out to think of you as Father . . . Mother . . . Goddess . . . or whatever. Please show me where all this fear is coming from' – such a prayer can begin a process of deep inner healing that will enable us to recognise both God and ourselves with clearer eyes.

When Bible readings or the daily office paint pictures of God or Jesus that feel uncomfortable or downright incredible to you, don't stuff your reaction; tell God about it. Ask God whether God really is the sort of person who would do such a thing. If you find praying to Jesus difficult, take your troubles with Jesus to Jesus himself. At the very least, the answers will convince you that God is different from, because immeasurably better than, any merely human person could ever be. Remember, when Job and the disciples and the saints pressed such questions, they saw wonderful things!

Third, getting to know God better will require us to experiment. If you've been praying in the same vein for years, maybe it's time – say once a week – to put yourself in the presence of God and then deliberately and explicitly address God with that metaphor you've been flirting with . . . if you're brave, take one that scares you silly. Try it, then offer God the somersaulted feelings, describe the men-as-trees-walking that you see! God will help you sort them out, make appropriate distinctions, suggest new experiments, startle you with the height and depth, the length and breadth of God.

The main point of these manoeuvres is to take down our defences, the barriers we erect against knowing God, other people, and ourselves. The aim, that is, is to open ourselves to God, to God incarnate, to the blessed Trinity who really know the answer to our question, to God, the One whose presence will satisfy both now and evermore!

[Preached at St Augustine's-by-the-Sea, Santa Monica,
Easter V, 1990]

TWO

Holy Trinity: Divine Comedy

Moses was keeping the flock of his father-in-law Jethro, the priest of Midian; he led his flock beyond the wilderness, and came to Horeb, the mountain of God. There the angel of the LORD appeared to him in a flame of fire out of a bush; he looked, and the bush was blazing, yet it was not consumed. Then Moses said, 'I must turn aside and look at this great sight, and see why the bush is not burned up.' When the LORD saw that he had turned aside to see, God called to him out of the bush, 'Moses, Moses!' And he said, 'Here I am.' Then he said, 'Come no closer! Remove the sandals from your feet, for the place on which you are standing is holy ground.' He said further, 'I am the God of your father, the God of Abraham, the God of Isaac, and the God of Jacob.' And Moses hid his face, for he was afraid to look at God. (Exodus 3:1–6)

Now there was a Pharisee named Nicodemus, a leader of

the Jews. He came to Jesus by night and said to him, 'Rabbi, we know that you are a teacher who has come from God; for no one can do these signs that you do apart from the presence of God.' Jesus answered him, 'Very truly, I tell you, no one can see the kingdom of God without being born from above.' Nicodemus said to him, 'How can anyone be born after having grown old? Can one enter a second time into the mother's womb and be born?' Jesus answered, 'Very truly, I tell you, no one can enter the kingdom of God without being born of water and Spirit. What is born of the flesh is flesh, and what is born of the Spirit is spirit. You must not be astonished that I said to you, "You must be born from above." The wind blows where it chooses, and you hear the sound of it, but you do not know where it comes from or where it goes. So it is with everyone who is born of the Spirit.' Nicodemus said to him, 'How can these things be?' Jesus answered him, 'Are you a teacher of Israel, and yet you do not understand these things?

'Very truly, I tell you, we speak of what we know and testify to what we have seen; yet you do not receive our testimony. If I have told you about earthly things and you do not believe, how can you believe if I tell you about heavenly things? No one has ascended into heaven except the one who descended from heaven, the Son of Man. And just as Moses lifted up the serpent in the wilderness, so must the Son of Man be lifted up, that whoever believes in him may have eternal life.

'For God so loved the world that he gave his only Son, so that everyone who believes in him may not perish but may have eternal life.' (John 3:1–16)

Trinity Sunday, our assigned propers pull on us one of the oldest tricks in the spiritual director's book: all try to startle us out of our spiritual stupor by thrusting us into the tension of puzzle and paradox: unconsumed burning bushes; born-again adults; poisonous serpents lifted up to heal; crucified Messiah; and finally, holy Trinity, Great One in Three!

Seemingly, the liturgical timing couldn't be worse! This is the first weekend of summer. Our minds have just disengaged from the year's problem-solving intensity. Like Moses keeping sheep in the midday desert, eyes staring blankly through rising heat waves, half closed against the monotonous sandy glare, we semiconsciously glimpse the invitation to theological adventure. But a little voice tells us, 'We've earned the right to dismiss it. Surely well-articulated explanations are stored on our hard disks under "Sunday School" or "catechism", or at least in dusty books in the Divinity School library. We know where to look them up if we ever need to. But do we? Didn't Bernard of Clairvaux forbid Cistercians to preach on this day, because the holy Trinity is a mystery beyond human telling?'

Just your luck to draw a *philosophical* theologian as preacher this morning! Not to worry! My professorial question is simple: have you ever considered that the doctrine of holy Trinity is a Divine joke?

Jokes surprise, amuse by exploiting ambiguities, misfitting things together. They also *instruct* by exposing the cracks in our elaborate facades of propriety. We try to impose order and decorum on public and private, even cosmic worlds. The truth is, it's all too big and messy for us to straighten out. Jokes remind us that human life is a comedy, that people – well, we – are funny, relentlessly attempting the impossible. And we are always at our silliest when we put on our Sunday best, don pious expressions, speak in tones of extreme unction, and pretend to tell the truth about God!

Where the holy Trinity is concerned, we have all been *so* serious, the Divine wit so subtle, that it's been easy to miss the punch line. This is embarrassing, because the incongruity is right on the surface in the words 'holy Trinity', in our beliefs about God!

On the one hand, 'holy' means 'cut off', 'separate'. Applied to God, it is a gasp of awe at the unutterable uniqueness of Divinity: this One is so unlike all others, that even for cherubim and seraphim, creatures who know God best, there is nothing better to say: 'Holy, holy, holy!' Such a God, we feel, must dwell in a world of his own, approachable at most by favoured servants, in secret inner sanctums, under protection of faultlessly performed liturgies!

How many Bible stories warn, more than any cosmic ray gun, naked Divinity is dangerous to a creature's health! Remember how Sinai/Horeb trembled, quaked, coughed up fire and smoke when YHWH descended with the Law, how God warned the people to wash their clothes, abstain from women, not even get close to his holy mountain. Despite the best of intentions, Divinity leaps out to strike Uzzah dead when he puts forth his hand to steady the slipping ark of the covenant. Earlier, Moses' own situation had become maximally precarious, when – following the mindlessly munching flocks – he unwittingly trespassed on Divine turf. Before God's other plans for Moses can go forward, the cleansing shoe-removal ritual has to be prescribed. Likewise, God instructs that gold bells be sewn around the hem of Aaron's priestly robes, to ring when Aaron ascends the altar steps, a signal for God to draw back lest Aaron die.

Yet, God's joke is on us: for the Bible also tells us, and we are deeply convinced, that God is *personal,* and we know from human experience how it is impossible to be personal all by oneself! No, baby selves awaken to an environment of tender loving care, focus around the centre of a mother's face. Interacting with father, sister, teacher, colleague, friend, lover brings out new dimensions of nature and character. Personal bonding is important to us, because our sense of who we are is not something we *contain* in isolation; rather it hangs web-like in-between. Moreover, it takes two to tango: you can't make me your partner without doing a different dance step yourself. Again, opposites attract for a reason: for if we begin life by imitating mom or dad, big brother or Aunt Maude, the truth is that we can all learn to dance to a wild variety of rhythms. The full beauty of each person comes to flower only through cross-fertilisation with others very different from ourselves.

Now if God really is personal, God can't be some giant buddha in the sky contemplating his navel! The cherubim and seraphim already dropped the hint when they sang, 'Holy, holy, holy', *three* times. No, if God is personal from eternity, there must be more than one, so that They can become who they are in relation one to another. Father-Mother God identifies herself as parent only in relation to his offspring, who recognises itself as Deity in response.

We know, too, how love is *ec-static*. Reaching, stretching out for the Beloved, the Lover expands, increases in size; the more there is to the Lover, the greater his magnetic power to pull the Beloved into being. Such mutual exchange is so high-energy, if you confine it to a symbiotic duo, it will self-destruct or explode. Precisely because Divine Love is fertile, creative, it overflows to welcome another into the heavenly household! And so it was impossible for God to be a loner. No, from eternity, by God's very nature, God is a dancing circle of unique persons, each pouring out itself to enrich, each becoming itself by loving others different and distinct from itself!

All the same, cherubim and seraphim sing a *holy* Trinity? Isn't this Divine *ménage à trois* the true upper-class society, living in an exclusive neighbourhood, dining only in the best clubs, somehow above mixing it up with ordinary folk except (as in the last campaign) when TV cameras are watching?

Once again, the Divine joke is on us. Not that Godhead isn't interesting enough to keep the Trinity eternally happy. Definitely, it is. They don't want to turn heaven into a gated community because they don't want to miss out on us, and what we would bring out in themselves. We know, it is one thing to try to understand what it's like to be someone else our own age, from our own culture, tastes and background; more difficult to see the world through the eyes of a small child, with the delights and fears of someone of different race, creed or national origin. Now I ask you, would the blessed Trinity offer us a challenge it hadn't first pioneered? Scarcely!

When the blessed Trinity fell in love with the human race, built the material world to be our home, it couldn't stand to keep out of any room; it flooded the whole earth with Divine glory! God the Son became one of us to make communication easier, Holy Spirit surrounds like air breathing each person into being.

And so God winks every time we call him 'holy', smiles at his funny people once more underestimating the social gap. Real Godhead can't be imprisoned in a throne room like the King of Siam or confined to a tiny tabernacle box (although, to be sure, God *is* really there). Divine Royalty is too curious to be exclusive, wants everybody at its party, sets a table wide enough for everyone to be an honoured guest. Blessed Trinity is fascinated, implants herself in every person. God in you brings out the good in me, God in me reaches out to touch and warm another. Divine humour lures us into mutual involvement, even across cultures into eventual harmony, warns how cutting others off is sure to shrink us!

The funny thing is, Divine Being can't be literally holy. God's very nature explodes the meaning of that word. Who God is makes it impossible for God or any of us to be separate or isolated, ever. And that, my friends, is a good joke!

[Preached at Trinity Church, Hollywood,
Trinity Sunday, 1993]

THREE

God, the Unfair!

When God saw what they did, how they turned from their evil ways, God changed his mind about the calamity that he had said he would bring upon them; and he did not do it.

But this was very displeasing to Jonah, and he became angry. He prayed to the LORD *and said, 'O* LORD*! Is not this what I said while I was still in my own country? That is why I fled to Tarshish at the beginning; for I knew that you are a gracious God and merciful, slow to anger, and abounding in steadfast love, and ready to relent from punishing. And now, O* LORD*, please take my life from me, for it is better for me to die than to live.' And the* LORD *said, 'Is it right for you to be angry?' Then Jonah went out of the city and sat down east of the city, and made a booth for himself there. He sat under it in the shade, waiting to see what would become of the city.*

The LORD *God appointed a bush, and made it come up*

over Jonah, to give shade over his head, to save him from his discomfort; so Jonah was very happy about the bush. But when dawn came up the next day, God appointed a worm that attacked the bush, so that it withered. When the sun rose, God prepared a sultry east wind, and the sun beat down on the head of Jonah so that he was faint and asked that he might die. He said, 'It is better for me to die than to live.'

But God said to Jonah, 'Is it right for you to be angry about the bush.' And he said, 'Yes, angry enough to die.' Then the LORD said, 'You are concerned about the bush, for which you did not labour and which you did not grow; it came into being in a night and perished in a night. And should I not be concerned about Nineveh, that great city, in which there are more than a hundred and twenty thousand persons who do not know their right hand from their left, and also many animals? (Jonah 3:10—4:11)

'For the kingdom of heaven is like a landowner who went out early in the morning to hire labourers for his vineyard. After agreeing with the labourers for the usual daily wage, he sent them into his vineyard. When he went out about nine o'clock, he saw others standing idle in the marketplace; and he said to them, "You also go into the vineyard, and I will pay you whatever is right." So they went. When he went out again about noon and about three o'clock, he did the same. And about five o'clock he went out and found others standing around; and he said to them, "Why are you standing here idle all day?" They said to him, "Because no one has hired us." He said to them, "You also go into the vineyard." When evening came, the owner of the vineyard said to his manager,

"Call the labourers and give them their pay, beginning with the last and then going to the first." When those hired about five o'clock came, each of them received the usual daily wage. Now when the first came, they thought they would receive more; but each of them also received the usual daily wage. And when they received it, they grumbled against the landowner, saying, "These last worked only one hour, and you have made them equal to us who have borne the burden of the day and the scorching heat." But he replied to one of them, "Friend, I am doing you no wrong; did you not agree with me for the usual daily wage? Take what belongs to you and go; I choose to give to this last the same as I give to you. Am I not allowed to do what I choose with what belongs to me? Or are you envious because I am generous?" So the last will be first, and the first will be last.'

(Matthew 20:1–16)

Today's propers lay a trap for us. Two great stories evoke our deep, even desperate interest in fairness, only to slap us with the judgement that *God is against it.* These lessons proclaim in so many words, what we always suspected: *God is unfair!* They not merely threaten, they catch us in the act of opposing God!

In the story of Jonah, the Ninevites are no mere stock characters, urban participants in a wicked pagan lifestyle. To Israel, they are paradigm case oppressors. Ninevah was the capital of Assyria, the empire that destroyed the Northern Kingdom, hauled God's people off into exile. A modern version would cast Jews as missionaries to Hitler's inner circle, or Iraqi

Christians to the United States government, to the
diplomatic corps and the CIA. The story packs a
double punch: first, it says that God so loves history's
worst villains that he is willing to forgive and forget if
they repent; and second, that God so longs to draw us
into his purposes, that he wants members of the now
delivered minority to love the oppressor, even become
agents of his pardon. Ninevah repented, God relented,
and that great city enjoyed his favour, just as if they had
been obedient all along. The author is on God's side,
portraying Jonah's outrage comically as a childish
tantrum. But aren't you even a little tempted to sym-
pathise with Jonah? After all, how can God love the
Jews and forgive Hitler? Jonah has a sense of fairness,
even if God does not!

The gospel presents a farm labour situation: some
workers slaved, bent over from morning til night,
sweltered under the noonday sun. But their wages were
the same as those who came at day's end. In California,
you could get reported to the Board of Unfair Labor
Practices for that. Besides, didn't the 1990s witness the
collapse of socialist economies that tried to do without
the profit motive and worker-incentive plans?

Closer to home, there was Matthew's church. Some
members had made large sacrifices for the sake of the
Gospel – eviction from their families, loss of jobs and
social position, threats of death and imprisonment.
Were new members, who now signed on in fairer
weather, who had not sweated blood to build the institution, really to receive the same reward? (And by
the way, what is St Augustine's version of this story?)

Or take women's ordination . . . Those pioneers who

spoke out and rocked the boat were battered and brutalised by the very Church they longed to serve. And now there comes a second generation, who take it all for granted, less confrontational, more easily accepted . . .

It isn't fair!

Our reactions show us the range of our demands. We insist not only that people don't get treated *worse* than they deserve (a denarius is a day's pay, a fair wage), but also that they don't get *better* than they deserve; not merely that like cases be treated alike (equal pay for equal work), but also that different cases should be treated differently. Our hearts insist that God make a difference between the innocent and the guilty, the diligent and the lazy, between foul weather and sunshine loyalties. We demand differentiation between our in-group and other out-groups; within our communities, a demarcation between outstanding and average, between good and bad. We want our society to be this way, we want our church to be this way, we want international politics to be this way, and – last but not least – we demand that the Kingdom of God be this way!

But why? Why are we so interested in fairness? Do we really want a penny-pinching providence to treat us exactly as we deserve? Have you never shuddered to think you might really get what was coming to you?

The point is, we all *do* shudder, and that's our clue: our obsession with fairness is premised on the empirically plausible fear that the necessities of life are in short supply: not enough food and shelter, space and time, energy and attention, not enough life and love to go around. Children starving in the Sudan tell us so, homeless people on our streets, unemployed waiting on the corners, substance abuse and gang wars, doctors' offices filled with the clinically depressed, even those painful and panicky corners of our own hearts agree that it is so. Where survival is chancy, chaos threatens. We need to believe there is something we can do to make sure we are numbered among the winners. The commitment to cosmic fairness provides one recipe: goods for the good, evils for the evil; therefore be good that the short supply of blessings may come your way. God's mercy to the wicked, his generosity to those who strive less hard, is threatening thrice over: in a climate of scarcity, it uses up capital needed to reward the virtuous. Moreover, if God is not following a policy of fairness, our limited energies have been misdirected. Worst of all, it hints that there may be nothing we can do to guarantee our share!

Why aren't we right in our concern for fairness? How can the tidings that God is unfair be anything but *Bad News*?

First of all, fairness is an approximate good. By this, I mean that it is probably the best policy that we humans could collectively hope to achieve. It *is* a good rule for our common life. Because the resources we control *are* scarce, we almost never succeed in treating one group better than it deserves without treating another worse than it deserves. This was true when the prophets preached YHWH's concern for a just society, and it is true now. That is why working for social justice is part of our individual and collective vocation.

When prophets look forward to a utopia where justice rolls down like waters, we can expect that the Kingdom of God will be no worse than just.

Second, to begin to see how Divine unfairness can be good news for us, we need to remember that we do not always wear the white hats. As Americans and Europeans we are rapacious, buying our unprecedented standard of living at developing countries' expense. As individuals, we have *done* as well as suffered terrible things, and we know the relief of God's gracious welcome.

More fundamentally, it makes no sense for God to be interested in fairness or desert, because God and creatures are incommensurate. God is so big and we are so tiny that we are almost nothing. There is nothing we could do or be, even if we were morally perfect, that could give us a *right* to God's attention, much less love. In relation to God, all differences among human beings shrink down to nothing. Expecting God to be interested in invidious distinctions among us would be like our judging the ladybugs to see which had paid us appropriate honour! It's silly, simply silly!

The bottom line, turning bad news to good, is that God governs the world from a position of abundance. The blessed Trinity *know* they are able to benefit each and every one of us far beyond anything we could desire or deserve, because God's own self is *Good* unsurpassable, and intimacy with God will satisfy. God's eye isn't on the ball of treating like cases alike and different cases differently. God's aim is higher: to create all things and stuff them with blessing, full to bursting. Even if God makes infinitely many of us, even if – as promised – we all last for ever, the wine will never run out, nor the manna fail.

Today's lessons are a sharp sword driving home the double-sided truth: that blessing, pressed down and running over, is guaranteed to us; *and* that the necessities of life are ultimately beyond our control. They target the most common mistake of religious people, warn that the attempt to *deserve* what can only be received as God's gracious gift will bend us disastrously out of shape. I'll say it again: check out your feelings about fairness. They could mean *you*!

[Preached at St Augustine's-by-the-Sea,
23 September 1990]

FOUR

Crucified God:
Abuser or Redeemer?

When I came to you, brothers and sisters, I did not come proclaiming the mystery of God to you in lofty words or wisdom. For I decided to know nothing among you except Jesus Christ, and him crucified. And I came to you in weakness and in fear and in much trembling. My speech and my proclamation were not with plausible words of wisdom, but with a demonstration of the Spirit and of power, so that your faith might rest not on human wisdom but on the power of God.

Yet among the mature we do speak wisdom, though it is not a wisdom of this age or of the rulers of this age, who are doomed to perish. But we speak God's wisdom, secret and hidden, which God decreed before the ages for our glory. None of the rulers of this age understood this; for if they had, they would not have crucified the Lord of glory. But, as it is written,

'What no eye has seen, nor ear heard,

nor the human heart conceived, what God has
prepared for those who love him'—
these things God has revealed to us through the Spirit; for
the Spirit searches everything, even the depths of God. For
what human being knows what is truly human except the
human spirit that is within? So also no one comprehends
what is truly God's except the Spirit of God.

(1 Corinthians 2:1–11)

It's always a philosopher's luck to get such a passage. It
ranks right down there with Colossians 2:8: 'See to it
that no one makes a prey of you by philosophy and
empty deceit!' But it's not only philosophers who have
a problem with today's epistle. St Paul's comment is
apt to provoke everyone's ambivalence. For on the one
hand, he must surely be right. Our Lord Jesus Christ is
Divine Wisdom incarnate, the Word spoken by God
before all things were made. Of all God's manifestations, our Lord Jesus Christ *crucified* is the most
telling.

And yet, St Paul knew that the cross was a scandal.
Popular Greek philosophy dismissed the mythology of
the immoral gods, lording it over humans, coming
down masked as creatures to rape women, to thwart
and torture human rivals; gods who could be bribed
with bloody sacrifices, who spoke in omens, oracles and
the entrails of birds. Epicureans deplored such stories
for cultivating fear and superstition, urged people to
ignore them, devote themselves to leading virtuous
lives. To them, the bloody sacrifice of Christ crucified
was one more unworthy tale. Likewise, Levitical law

ruled that anyone who died by hanging from a tree was cursed, definitively cut off from God and his people. Only logical that Jews should take crucifixion as conclusive proof that Jesus was not God's Messiah.

And what about us? Dare we admit that Christ crucified is a picture of abuse? *The cross of Christ exposes our vulnerability to abuse*: to physical and sexual violence within the home, between parents and children, spouses and lovers. The cross of Christ is a symbol of the way human lives are counted for nothing – not only in Serbia and Rwanda, in Afghanistan and Iraq, but everywhere and always, right here and right now. The cross of Christ is an exposé of how people are battered, tortured and disposed of; of how life and creativity are crushed out of us, on a mere whim, out of meanness, fear or sheer greed. The cross of Christ is an outward and visible sign of caricatured, crippled, bound and distorted humanity, the work of all those forces that keep us from being who we were meant to be.

Likewise, the cross of Christ exposes the ease with which we become abusers. Did you ever notice how when you're hurting, you're more apt to fly off the handle at little things, to swear at the traffic? That little snapshot of how hurt brings us to blasphemy, enlarges into a picture of the general human condition. Beat a child, abandon him, starve her for affection, day in and day out – is it any surprise you get a gangland adolescent who shoots up with drugs and kills for the sport of it? Stories say that Hitler's father tied him to a tree and beat him every night. And even when we don't lay a hand on one another, the sins of the fathers and mothers readily descend to the children, spread out to spouses and colleagues as we unconsciously act out the fears and rage of our neurotic adaptations. The cross of Christ is a focused picture, not only of what abusers do to others; it is a grim portrait of what we the abused and abusive are doing to ourselves!

Elevating Christ crucified to a religious symbol, making the cross the centrepiece of our liturgical decoration seems to award such scandal the Divine seal of approval. For many, it raises the fear and superstition that God is a child-abuser: after all, did he not *make* his Son Jesus suffer? Can we not identify with Jesus in the Garden with loud cries and tears, only to submit like an adaptive child to the Father's hostile will? Does not the cross, with its commission to imitative discipleship, send the message that God is determined to let life and the world batter and bend us until we are unfit for his presence, and then cast us off as vile worthless things? Does this not make God the pioneer and patron of present oppressors, who anyhow act as if they rule by Divine right and with Divine blessing?

Taking such messages really to heart would drive us to rebel against God, symbolically to kill him by embracing atheism. Instead, many of us become polarised, maintaining our religious alliances on the surface, burying our wounds and anger ever more deeply within.

Truth to tell, we do not know *why* God permits abuse. In part, it seems an inevitable consequence of what it is to be human. But I invite you to an exercise of deep spiritual intimacy: take this question directly to God, and watch what she shows you!

What we do know, the Good News that even philosophy will tell you, is that it's impossible for God to be a child-abuser, because God's very nature is Love. When God utters his Word in Christ crucified, he is not speaking the language of our fearful psychological projections, but a new and heavenly tongue. The key to its interpretation is the identity of the one who suffers: viz., God himself.

Christ crucified does not represent an extra-punitive God taking his rage out on a handy target, or even God making the innocent take the rap for the guilty because justice demands that someone must pay. Rather, first of all, the broken, bleeding, naked, defecating body of Jesus is an outward and visible sign of the agony God feels for us and with us in his Divine nature, has felt by anticipation from before the foundations of the world.

Second, God so loves our human nature that he is not content to suffer only in his Divine nature, whose infinite capacity is rich with other things. No, God determined to be one of us, take to himself our whole nature – a body that could be tortured, a mind that could be blown by unbearable pain; a psyche that could be gripped by fear, tear and rip with desertions and betrayals; a physique that could break and die. God did it out of love, to identify with us in the worst that befalls us.

More radical still, God Almighty in Christ Jesus died by hanging from a tree to become ritually cursed for us, to identify himself with the whole range of human blasphemy: not only with Hitlers and Stalins, with drug-pushers and sweat-shop owners, with child-abusers and wife-beaters; but also with those dark pockets of our souls which are so hurt and angry that they curse God and wish for death, with those closets of rage seemingly nuclear in proportion which we unconsciously turn to self-torture.

God in Christ Jesus makes the cross his throne of judgement, exposes the worst the Powers of Darkness can do, draws us a picture of every human being – victimised and brutalising, in wish or deed, both self and others.

But God in Christ crucified, God killed and cursed, relentlessly sanctifying both victim and blasphemer with his presence, defeats his enemies with the Gospel that *nothing*, no *nothing*, can separate us from his love and power.

God in Christ crucified, that very Power and Wisdom of God, is God for us and God with us . . . a God we can believe in . . . a God we can glory in . . . a God we can love!

[Preached at St Augustine's-by-the-Sea,
Epiphany V, 1990]

FIVE

Curse and Promise

After these things the word of the LORD came to Abram in a vision, 'Do not be afraid, Abram, I am your shield; your reward shall be very great.' But Abram said, 'O Lord GOD, what will you give me, for I continue childless, and the heir of my house is Eliezer of Damascus?' And Abram said, 'You have given me no offspring, and so a slave born in my house is to be my heir.' But the word of the LORD came to him, 'This man shall not be your heir; no one but your very own issue shall be your heir.' He brought him outside and said, 'Look toward heaven and count the stars, if you are able to count them.' Then he said to him, 'So shall your descendants be.' And he believed the LORD; and the LORD reckoned it to him as righteousness.

Then he said to him, 'I am the LORD who brought you from Ur of the Chaldeans, to give you this land to possess.' But he said, 'O Lord GOD, how am I to know that I shall possess it?' He said to him, 'Bring me a heifer three years old, a female goat three years old, a ram three years old, a turtledove, and a young pigeon.' He brought him all these and cut them in two, laying each half over against the other; but he did not cut the birds in two. And when birds of prey came down on the carcasses, Abram drove them away.

As the sun was going down, a deep sleep fell upon Abram, and a deep and terrifying darkness descended upon him . . .

When the sun had gone down and it was dark, a smoking fire pot and a flaming torch passed between these pieces. On that day the LORD *made a covenant with Abram, saying, 'To your descendants I give this land . . .'*

(Genesis 15:1–12, 17–18)

YHWH the extravagant promiser, Abram the eager believer went back a long way. Abram was 75 years old when God propositioned him in Haran: 'Leave home! Go to the land which I will show you.' Like all lovers, YHWH dangled future bounty. First, he would make Abram famous – nations would be blessed or cursed in proportion as they were friend or foe to Abram's clan; all families of the earth would bless themselves in him. Second, God promised the land of Canaan where Abram's posterity could spread out, settle down, like post-war suburbanites in San Fernando Valley orange groves. Kissed by Divine presence, Abram agreed, pulled up stakes, and became a pilgrim.

Mostly, life went well. Abram got rich, his flocks and herds fruitful and multiplying. His career featured world travel – even turned a profit on foreign adventure when Pharaoh took 'sister' Sarai as one of his wives, only to be visited with Divine plagues and pave Abram's way out of town with gold! Abram grew into the virtues of a powerful patron – generously allowing Lot the greener pastures; marshalling military might and cunning to rescue cities, liberate kidnapped kin. Unwittingly reaching down the centuries, Abram paid tithes to Melchizedek, King of Peace, priest for ever, offering bread and wine. At Shechem, at Bethel, at the oaks of Mamre, where Abram pitched tents and built altars to the Lord, there were intimate rendezvous, YHWH still full of promises, Abram still a childless nomad, resting his head on borrowed ground.

And so, *after* Abram's victorious battle, YHWH God of armies shows up: 'Fear not, Abram, I am your shield; your reward will be very great!' Same story every time. Now Abram sighs: 'What will you give me?' Wealth and power are but temporary, fleeting advantage without offspring to remember one's good name. Ever the charmer, YHWH distracts Abram's attention to the stars, and declares, 'Your descendants will be as many as that.' Now reluctant, Abram still *believed* God, and this time it was reckoned to him as righteousness.

YHWH presses his luck, repeats the second promise, his credibility already stretched and strained: 'O Lord God, how am I to know that I shall be a land-holder?' Talk is cheap. Time's a wasting. Ritual reassurance, covenant-sealing ceremony, love affair gone legitimate, official business deal. Heifer, she-goat, ram, split down the middle; turtle dove and pigeon, necks wrung. Sundown, trance, dread and darkness. Smoking fire pot, flaming torch and fiery pillar passing through the pieces.

YHWH taking on himself the conditional curse of covenant vows. How sure are YHWH's promises? 'Let it be to me as it is with these animals if I do not keep my word!'

The fact is we are Abram. And Lent calls us to candour about our relationship with God. For God has made a covenant with creation, lured us with extravagant promises of fruitfulness and turf.

God promises not just that our lives will be bearable, something we can scratch our way through, hanging on by our fingernails . . . not simply that it will be punctuated with enjoyments, even successive accomplishments, tenuously threaded like beads on a string. God promises us fruitfulness, that what we do and suffer here and now will count for something . . . not just for something or other, but something galaxy-size! And God also promises place and time, our very own room to stretch and try our wings, soil in which to sow and water our seeds until they burst into flower.

And then we wait, our whole lives threatening to yawn between promise and fulfilment. We lower our standards, set our hopes on Ishmael. Blessed the one who wanders with Abram through an enviable mix of satisfaction and frustration, of adventure and boredom, disappointments and success. Life here can be good while it lasts, between Mozart and sunshine, chocolate and tennis, flowers, a few friends, an occasional lover's kiss. *But if what we see is what we get, wasn't it perverse of God to raise our hopes for more?*

For many, life is more sinister, already before sundown cloaked with terror and deep dread. Sometimes there isn't enough love or money, food or housing, jobs or health care to go around. Even in our rich country, people go hungry or live on the street. Some of us are just so original – dare I say 'queer' – that there's nowhere we can fit in and be ourselves at the same time. Some are uprooted by family violence, hate crimes, and war. Sometimes we have been so desperate, need and hurt so much, that we have done terrible things to others, defacing the image of God in all concerned. We are strangers, exiles. Victims and victimising, we keep moving, wandering. We really need that homeland whose builder and maker is God!

How often do we find ourselves on the edge, where we can scarcely stand it any longer . . . unable to identify with prosperous Abram losing patience, feeling more like those hacked-in-two animals, almost too far gone to cry, 'What will you give me, O Lord? Hurry up, before there's no me left to give it to!'

Now Abram's God and ours is YHWH God Almighty: this God can shield, protect us, after it's already too late. Abram's God and ours is All and Only Wise: no problem is insuperable; Stumped-by-Nothing is God's name!

And Abram's God and ours has two answers. Looking down on hacked-up pieces, the predictable Divine invitation: 'Fetch them here, bring them as an offering to me!' Darkness and dread close in, hover. But suddenly their power is broken by Christ crucified, that flaming torch and fiery pillar, shining on with unquenchable light: 'Let it be to me as it is now with these my brothers and sisters, because I did not fulfil my promise in their time.' God in Christ crucified absorbs the curse – caricatured, distorted, ruined, hacked in two by others' rage. And God in Christ

59

crucified *becomes* blasphemy, casting his lot with the enemies of God, with those who wreck and ruin others.

God in Christ crucified passes through our world, through the worst we can suffer, be or do; passes through as flaming torch and fiery pillar, light splitting dread and darkness, taking final eternal-lifetime vows: *'I AM Emmanuel-God, with you no matter what, all the time!'*

Nor does Abram's God and ours stop with 'Misery loves company!' Ever extravagant, God in Christ crucified numbers us children in Abram's bosom. It is to us already battered and broken by self and others, to moulded clay on the verge of resolving into dust again, it is to us that God promises immeasurable fruitfulness, boundless turf!

Holy Eucharist is the ritual that tells us so. Here we offer ourselves, souls and bodies, our weary waiting, broken dreams, the hurt we suffered, the grief we've caused. Here with broken bread and poured out wine we show forth Christ crucified, that flaming torch and fiery pillar, passing through not over, consuming the sacrifice, turning it, us, into Christ's *glorified* body, into God's own self.

Abram was 100 years old, Sarah 90, when the ridiculous happened and Isaac finally came. Frustrating as it is, Abram's God and ours will doubtless continue to take his own sweet time. Holy Eucharist is meant to reassure, convince us: the promises of God are as sure as Christ crucified, as eternal in the heavens as God's own self!

[Preached at Trinity Church, Hollywood,
Lent II, 1995]

SIX

King of Peace

'Blessed is he who comes in the name of the Lord!' 'Peace
on earth, and joy in the highest!'
(The Passion according to Matthew)

We have just re-enacted our Lord's triumphal entry,
God's Messiah riding into Jerusalem on a donkey, fulfilling Zechariah's prophecy, inaugurating the Reign of
God, a government of stable, universal, everlasting
peace.

Deep down, we all long for peace. What parents
wouldn't like to get the family through dinner without
a fight? What administrator doesn't long for harmo-
nious employee relations? Which rector doesn't pray
for the parish to forego sibling rivalry, live together in
brotherly and sisterly love? *We all long for peace, but we*
don't know how to get it. World leaders daily sound the

rhetoric, only to watch ethnic conflicts erupt like boils in yet another part of the globe.

We do the best we can. We try to civilise ourselves with a veneer of good manners. We teach the children to say 'please' and 'thank you'. We learn which are the safe subjects of conversation. We develop antiseptic ways of expressing disagreements. As much as possible we keep a lid on our emotions. And don't forget the religious etiquette that we so meticulously observe (and don't get me wrong, I love it as much as anyone else) – the *Book of Common Prayer* that so structures our worship that we don't have to deal with what anyone else is really thinking or feeling.

Etiquette does smooth the way, enable us to tolerate each other enough to get a job done or keep the family together until the children are grown. But it is peace of limited scope, because it is based on cover-up. What are we going to do with all the anger, anxiety and resentment stuffed down behind our polite workplace smiles? Take it out on the people we live with? Let it seep out in sarcasm? Jog, chop wood, weed for all we're worth? Keep it all under wraps until one day we explode? Close down so effectively as to commit emotional suicide? *Our peace isn't comprehensive and it can't last.*

King Jesus rode into Jerusalem on Palm Sunday to launch his decisive attack on the real enemy of peace, whose name is Death. Now, King Jesus was not born yesterday. He knew that ever since Eden humans have faced life-threatening forces on the *outside* – earthquakes, famines, winds, floods. But he came to expose the more insidious fact that fallen human nature as we know and *are* it, has a built-in bias towards Death.

Biologists tell us that catabolism works right alongside metabolism: at every moment of our lives, some biological forces are at work to build up bodily tissue, while others labour to tear it down. And although God intended our souls to transcend the merely animal, Freud was not far wrong to say that psyche mirrors biology: every instinct we have that drives towards love and life is matched by an opposite force that pushes towards hatred and death. In fact, the two intertwine, make us experts at hitting upon actions that express both instincts at once. Even the life-preserving activity of eating is hostile: you destroy what you eat! Or how about the father whose workaholic efforts to support the family produce alienation that breaks both the family and his own health? Or what about social programmes to feed the hungry, which result in increased population and more starvation? These ironies are tragic: from a merely human point of view, the forces of Death have the last word.

Most of the time, we can't bear to face self-destructive forces within ourselves. We prefer to deny them, displace our fear and anger at internal sources of ruin onto external scapegoats. 'It is not I who am dangerous to my own health; it is those others.' Even others like me would put the menace too close to home. So we blame people of other races, ethnic or linguistic groups, or people with a different political or theological or sexual orientation. We tell ourselves that if only *they* were removed from the scene, 'the world would be safe for democracy'. The truth is that if today's enemies vanished, we would have to invent others, lest we recognise the enemy Death at work within.

King Jesus knew he could not be King of Everlasting Peace, unless he came first as King of Righteousness and Truth, to expose the obstacles to peace rooted in each and every human heart. He began his ministry by contradicting the defensive separatist tendencies of the most religious people, the Pharisees. He ate with tax-collectors, forgave prostitutes, welcomed the lame, the halt and the blind into God's Kingdom, to proclaim the good news that everybody will be safe but nobody will be left out in the Realm of God. His actions and parables dramatised forgiveness and inclusiveness, pressured the self-righteous to recognise their own inner bias towards hatred and death. When nothing else worked, King Jesus launched a direct attack on their mile-thick fortifications, called those 'pillars of piety' 'whitewashed sepulchres, full of dead bones'. Unsurprisingly, they made Jesus their new scapegoat: 'It is expedient that one man should die for the people.' Everything would be all right, if only he were dead!

And so King Jesus rode into Jerusalem for this last momentous battle with the real enemy of peace. When all else failed to produce self-knowledge, King Jesus courted a crisis, provoked them to act out their pent-up hostility on his own flesh. The torture they devised dripped with irony: death by hanging from a tree ritually accursed *the victim*, separated not only from life but from God. Yet this time, it cursed *the perpetrators*, turned the people of God into murderers of the Messiah whose way they so long prepared. The tormented, mutilated, cursed, dead body of King Jesus drew those good religious people . . . draws us . . . a vivid picture of our own dark sides. More than that, Christ crucified portrays on the outside the hateful cursing and devastation that we secretly execute on the inside, on our very own selves!

King Jesus reigned, King of Peace and King of Truth, from the throne of the cross. Anointed with myrrh and crowned with thorns, he reigned not only King of the Jews there present but of all people, at all times and places. High and lifted up, he broadcasts the Truth declared earlier in the desert: we humans cannot live by the bread of our own efforts. The forces of Love and Life within us are swamped by the powers of Hatred and Destruction. If Life and Love are to win in any of us, it will only be by that Word which proceeds from the mouth of God.

> *Sing, my tongue, the glorious battle! Sing the winning of the fray.*
> *Now above the cross, the trophy. Sound the high triumphal lay.*
> *Tell how Christ, the world's Redeemer, as a victim won the day! Amen.*

[Preached at Trinity Church, Hollywood, Palm Sunday, 1987]

SEVEN

Risen Dead,
Borrowed Life!

But on the first day of the week, at early dawn, they came to the tomb, taking the spices that they had prepared. They found the stone rolled away from the tomb, but when they went in, they did not find the body. While they were perplexed about this, suddenly two men in dazzling clothes stood beside them. The women were terrified and bowed their faces to the ground, but the men said to them, 'Why do you look for the living among the dead? He is not here, but has risen. Remember how he told you, while he was still in Galilee, that the Son of Man must be handed over to sinners, and be crucified, and on the third day rise again.' Then they remembered his words, and returning from the tomb, they told all this to the eleven and to all the rest. Now it was Mary Magdalene, Joanna, Mary the mother of James, and the other women with them who told this to the apostles. (Luke 24:1–10)

At the dawn of the week, at the dawn of the day, at the dawn of the age to come, the women venture forth with spices to pay homage, a last gesture of respect, one last touch, holding on just a little longer, before heat and worms do their inevitable work in darkness. Suddenly, they see! The stone is rolled away, the body replaced by two figures in blazing apparel! Terrified and trembling, the women drop to the ground, hide their face. No time for paralysis, 'He is risen!' 'Why look for the living among the dead!' 'Run off and be missionaries, hurry tell the male disciples, who incidentally won't believe you – just female hysteria – until they see him for themselves!'

Easter Good News? Or trite razzle dazzle, unearthly messengers, quaking earth, rolling stones, missing corpses, dead men walking? Now that Cecil B. DeMille is dead, this script wouldn't make the late night re-runs in today's Hollywood, with *Star Wars*, *Jurassic Park*, *Titanic*, and ever-escalating extravaganza special effects. Such *deus ex machina*, quick-fix scenarios barely qualify for grade-B movies, much less the substance of religion. Besides they raise more questions than they answer. If it's so easy for God, why didn't he do it before? Why not more often? Why not when it's really important? Such plot lines are too unsubtle for our tastes, because they gloss over the complex texture of our lives.

This reaction just goes to show why it's a bad idea to skim the beginning and end of a book – yes, that would be Christmas and Easter – while skipping over what comes in between. If we flip back two or three chapters, we find accounts of flimsy loyalties, wounded betrayals, desperate jealousy, disastrously distorted discernment, cowardly government, stories that dig down through fear and hatred to the human core, that teeter-totter between life and death. Easter's message is meant to resolve that plot, and so to be relevant to turn-of-the twenty-first-century human beings.

Still, we are the jaded generation! Even Death is a subject that *has to be proved* interesting! Considered simply as an end, like a punctuation mark randomly dropped on a pages-long run-on sentence, Death would not be any more loaded than a mere beginning. Recall the Epicurean philosopher who reasoned, 'If we aren't anxious about the fact that there were times *before* we existed, why should we be upset at the idea that time will go on *after* us?'

Part of the answer is that Death has meaning because *our lives have shape, and Death shapes our lives.* For we human beings are personal *animals*, who trace an animal life cycle, upwards from birth through growth towards our prime, downwards through decline and diminishment towards death. Moreover, this movement is driven by simultaneously operative opposing forces: metabolism that builds up, and catabolism that tears down. Normally, at first the life force predominates, then the destructive forces gain an ever-increasing advantage. Still, earthworms and robins don't make heavy weather of this. When Father Greer's dog died, he was very sad, but not for the dog of whom he reported, 'McGregor had a good life!'

Death looms large for us humans, because we are *personal* animals, and personal life has a forward thrust towards a future enriched by past and present. The shape of animal life 'runs interference' with us as persons with loving attachments, with aims and projects. When personality gets planted in animal nature, Death turns sinister, no longer a natural shaper but a poisoner of life. For as persons we search for, appreciate the significance of, what happens, we try to order our lives into patterns of positive meaning. Among other things, we can and do anticipate, ponder the prospect that one day we will go 'the way of all flesh'; one day, 'we will not be'. Our psycho-spiritual being is tied to the animal developmental process, so that we *experience* how every forward thrust of life means a death to the previous developmental stage, so that even our fullest flowering is underwritten by a history of losses – leaving mother's arms, from home to first grade, off to college, from one job to another up the corporate ladder.

If animal nature contains the seeds of its own demise, its life instinct hard-wires a fight-or-flight instinct to be triggered by stimuli from natural predators. In us personal animals, intelligence takes primal fear of Death and designs it into something far more baroque and insidious. Fear convinces us of half-truths – that the necessities of life must be scarce, our grip on them weak, or Death wouldn't be a threat. Both the Bible and experience tell how human vices grow in its soil. *Greed*, the hoarding of bulging surpluses to make sure we have enough. *Gluttonous consumption*, to make sure we occupy so much space that we can't be evicted. *Envy, jealousy, ruthless competition*, because merits mean entitlements and what you get comes off my plate. *Malicious gossip*, to detach others from the communities whose help we need. *Hatred, party spirit,* to fuel the fires of us against them. These grip our hearts to contaminate our relationships, distort our projects long before we die. At times we wonder how life can be worth living!

Easter replies, 'Because Somebody "up there" is ready, willing and able to raise the dead.' We repeat, 'So what? Quick-fix change at the end would land us in Milton's hell, for ever stuck in all our vices and dysfunctions, *unless* the resurrecting power could somehow reach back into the fabric of our lives to counter our desperation.' Easter claims that God can and does. But do we have any evidence, any experience of how this can be so?

Well, think back to the most terrifying experience of your life . . . when with or without the miracles of modern medicine your body literally didn't have strength to make a fist, when blood clotted the wrong way, infection raged out of control, when the damning diagnosis came – cancer, MS, multiple bypass, HIV . . . the mind-blowing panic of the swerving truck, the rage at your partner's divorce announcement, the paralysing fear at walking out of locked closets, or back into places haunted by failure and abuse, the leaden depression that descends, flattens when you lose and can't find another job or relationship. Re-member, re-enter those times when you were really convinced it was all over, when you were absolutely certain there was no power in you – body, mind, or spirit – strong enough to pull you together, enable you to stand.

But here you are, risen from the bed! You've got yourself to church on Easter Sunday, more or less clothed and in your right mind! There are at least two interpretations of this fact. Our head reasons, the feelings must have been misleading; we were a lot stronger than we thought! Sometimes, maybe. Easter turns this calculation upside down, urges us to face how often feelings told the truth. Left to itself, nature would *not* have recovered health, kept a grip on sanity, renewed us for human connection and productive lives. To whatever extent we are here, hale and sound, it is the work of some 'higher' miraculous power.

Easter confronts our primal fear of death with the truth that for each and every one of us the worst has already happened, not just once, but time and time again. We have already died, repeatedly. Recognised or not, the life to which we have risen is borrowed, 'hid with Christ in God'. The first step to Easter joy is explicit recognition – 'Mary!' 'Rabboni!' – a chosen intimacy with that power at work within us all along. The better we get to know each other, the more our daily deaths and resurrections reassure us that when we come to that big *dead*-line at the end, we will be dealing with a God who is experienced at putting Humpty Dumpties back together again!

But Easter joy will pour down, pervade, fill us brimful to overflowing, to the extent that we respond to its radical demand – to live as risen dead, every day, all the rest of our earthly lives. You see, it stands to reason, if the worst has already happened, not once, but repeatedly, we don't need to waste our energy and ingenuity contriving ways to avoid it. Not right away but one day, we will have crossed Jordan's verge so often, carried in Jesus' crucified and resurrected hands, we'll greet Death's many faces with 'ho, hum' recognition: 'Oh, so it's you again!' Not immediately but little by little, sinister vices will seem useless, life's poisons will drain, we will relax into loving co-operation with our Lord Jesus, the One who died and rose again! Less and less will we get sucked in, trapped in vicious dramas. More and more, we will look above, recognise ourselves already seated with him in glory, at God's right hand!

[Preached at St Thomas', New Haven,
Easter 1998]

EIGHT

Secure Dust

But the souls of the righteous are in the hand of God, and no torment will ever touch them. In the eyes of the foolish they seemed to have died, and their departure was thought to be a disaster, and their going from us to be their destruction; but they are at peace. For though in the sight of others they were punished, their hope is full of immortality. Having been disciplined a little, they will receive great good, because God tested them and found them worthy of himself; like gold in the furnace he tried them, and like a sacrificial burnt offering he accepted them. In the time of their visitation they will shine forth, and will run like sparks through the stubble. They will govern nations and rule over peoples, and the Lord will reign over them forever. Those who trust in him will understand truth, and the faithful will abide with him in love, because grace and mercy are upon his holy ones, and he watches over his elect. (Wisdom 3:1–9)

The cancer had done its work, first surreptitiously, hidden from view; then chomping out bodily parts, like a ravenous dog at Thanksgiving dinner. Little Andrew burst through the door, lightning-searched the house. 'Where's grandpa?' he demanded. 'When is he coming back?' But the family had lost its religion two generations before. 'He's never coming back,' the father replied, 'and we don't know where he is!'

Remember you are dust, and to dust you shall return.

The appalled undertaker wrung his hands, but they insisted on watching while workmen lowered the casket with straps and pulleys. Six, eight feet down, the roses sentimentally arranged, the tears and hand-prints, now the eyes reluctant to part with mortal remains of all she had meant to them. 'How can she breathe in there?' the little voice piped up. Straining to be clinical, the adult voice wobbled: 'She quit breathing when she died.'

Remember you are dust, and to dust you shall return.

The rector had winced, but Miracle Charlie got his way in the end. How many times had AIDS knocked him down, only to have him struggle, rise from the bed! But Charlie knew, this mortal coil isn't built to last. 'When I die, I want to be cremated. I want my ashes placed on a table in front of the altar with this autographed picture of my handsome smiling face beside it. Then plant a tree, pour my ashes into the hole so they can nourish its roots.' It was Hollywood after all, and Charlie was an actor. He had to go out with flair.

Remember you are dust, and to dust you shall return.

It had been a 'clean' relationship, unstained by guilt,

unsmeared by shame or regrets. For years, Pat and Sue had shared deeply of themselves – triumphs and troubles, sorrows and joys. Spiritual friends, they had exchanged notes on what they had learned about God, their trial-and-error experiments with prayer. Pat's death cut deep, tore away the veil between this world and wider life, pulled Sue along with her. Straddling both worlds, Sue *saw* how in comparison this world is shadow-play and flimsy; *experienced* how chunky and solid, how really real things are on the other side; for some days, *felt* them both held in God's eternal grip, inseparable for ever.

The souls of the righteous are in the hands of God!

We are here today, because to us, Death is no stranger. We are here today, because we *know* Death's power to do its work.

Death has already messed with our affairs . . . Robbed us of grandparents who loved us when kids teased at school and parents were too busy to care . . . Stolen mother's love or father's fun, leaving us alone to figure things out by ourselves. Death snatches away youth full of promise, on the verge of discovery; drugs, depression and disease lure the unsuspecting before their time. Death tears away friends and lovers when life is just beginning to gel, when roots have inter-locked and networked us into one flesh and spiritual partnership.

Many of us ourselves have had near misses . . . when blood pressure suddenly plummets while giving birth . . . when brakes fail, wheels roll off in fast and reckless traffic . . . when infection ravages the body before they discover what it is . . . when airport security almost doesn't x-ray that late bag a second time.

Even now, some of us are served with disturbing diagnoses, struggle now to avoid, now to take in the notion that our non-negotiable deadline may come much sooner than we think!

We are here because we have begun to understand why Paul hails Death our last enemy. Unfortunately, we also know Death's wiles, how she can torment, so caricature us in advance, that we actually welcome her embrace!

Oh yes! We remember, we are dust and to dust we shall return!

Death makes a mockery of us as persons, declares all that we are and do to be vanity and striving with the wind. 'I got my PhD, an Ivy League job.' *Remember you are dust and to dust you shall return.* 'I've fallen in love with someone special.' *Remember you are dust and to dust you shall return.* 'My salary broke six figures.' *Remember you are dust and to dust you shall return.* Like Satan, Death co-opts the Word of God, our Ash Wednesday liturgy, to tempt us with despair. 'Where is grandpa? When will he come back?' 'Nowhere and never!' *Remember, you are dust and to dust you shall return!*

We have gathered to contradict this testimony, come once again to celebrate our hope. We are here because we have tasted and seen Love-stronger-than-Death. Our faith is rooted in nothing more or less than God's character. Would the God who made all things from nothing, whose patience waited centuries to grow up the human race; would the God who became part of creation, joining Divine to human nature, the better to bind all things together in Godself; would this very God be content with four score years, Job-like lose sons and daughters with equanimity, so long as there were others in their place? What kind of Mother would God be not to grieve such loss according to his infinite capacity? What kind of Father would God be not to prevent it if she could?

Yes, the souls of the righteous are in the hand of God.

Death is no punishment for Adam's past sin, but a normal outworking of animal nature. It is because – like God – we are personal that death is an ordeal, challenging our bid for positive meaning. But God in Christ Jesus, Love-stronger-than-Death is our champion. God became human, let Death our enemy do its worst, put to death his Messianic pretensions, all to reassure us that when we die as much as when we live, God is with us.

Death cannot snatch us from his crucified hand!

Nor will Love-stronger-than-Death allow itself to be outdone. If omnivorous Death stuffs all into its maw for decomposition – *yes, we are dust, and to dust we shall return* – God our Re-Creator is equally ravenous, hungers and thirsts not only for the righteous but for the cursed and cursing, outcaste sinners for whom the world makes no room.

Everywhere and always, no matter what our condition, we are all, individually and together, eternally secure in God's crucified hand!

Yes, Love-stronger-than-Death has betrothed us, longs for consummation, that endless family reunion, the wedding feast of the Lamb! The blessed Trinity will not rest until our connections are re-established, until we enjoy intimacy as wholesome and fulfilling as theirs. Still, God in Christ crucified knows our human limitations, our incapacity to wait so long. Already, we are invited, have given our RSVPs. It is not too early to come. Already, we Christians mock Death, dissolve to dust, crying 'Alleluia, alleluia, alleluia!', rendezvous not at tombs but at holy Eucharist. Why seek the living among the dead? For here we are made members of Christ; and those we love are members of Christ. And we are together, alive for evermore!

Nothing can separate us from God's crucified hand!

[Preached at Christ Church, New Haven,
All Souls' Day, 1996]

PART TWO

Chosen Children, Daring Disciples

NINE

Immodest Proposal

*In the sixth month the angel Gabriel was sent by God to a
town in Galilee called Nazareth, to a virgin engaged to
a man whose name was Joseph, of the house of David. The
virgin's name was Mary. And he came to her and said,
'Greetings, favoured one! The Lord is with you.' But she
was much perplexed by his words and pondered what sort
of greeting this might be. The angel said to her, 'Do not
be afraid, Mary, for you have found favour with God.
And now, you will conceive in your womb and bear a son,
and you will name him Jesus. He will be great, and will
be called the Son of the Most High, and the Lord God will
give to him the throne of his ancestor David. He will
reign over the house of Jacob forever, and of his kingdom
there will be no end.' Mary said to the angel, 'How can
this be, since I am a virgin?' The angel said to her, 'The
Holy Spirit will come upon you, and the power of the Most
High will overshadow you; therefore the child to be born*

will be holy; he will be called Son of God. And now, your
relative Elizabeth in her old age has also conceived a son;
and this is the sixth month for her who was said to be
barren. For nothing will be impossible with God.' Then
Mary said, 'Here am I, the servant of the Lord; let it
be with me according to your word.' Then the angel
departed from her. (Luke 1:26–38)

Hail Mary, full of grace, the Lord is with thee!

Her birthday present was to tell him he was illegitimate, give him the name of the father he had never met. His facade-identity cracked releasing lava flows of shame. His run from pain bottoming into emptiness slowed to despair. Then he got a job teaching multicultural inner-city children, made his home room a non-abusive space to call their own, showed them how to live fair, to value themselves, respect each other. Alumni records tracked current addresses . . . Last week his father called, 40 years of wondering past, lost opportunities swallowed by new beginnings!

He shall be called Son of the Most High!

Midnight vigil, the air heavy with sweat and urine. Mother on the floor, at bed-foot, asleep with grief, her only son dying with AIDS. Suddenly, Tom woke with a start, whispered, 'I feel as if I'm giving birth to twins.' 'What would you name them?' I asked. 'Joshua and Elihu!' 'My little nephew Joshua has been three months in a coma. Maybe something good will come of this for him!'

Hail, Favoured One! Your fruit is Jesus!

'Momma! Momma Rufina! The soldiers just shot

my brother! Come, help me!' Instead, she wriggled deeper into the weeds, thorns tearing her flesh, hiding from that Salvadorean slaughter of innocents, soldiers butchering the entire village. Later, US officials wouldn't believe Rufina. Surely God didn't make wretched peasant women bearers of Truth!

He will put down the mighty from their seats, exalt the humble and meek!

His priesthood had nurtured many vocations; his stirring words, sacramental vision had torn curtains of despair, flung open windows of hope, taught hundreds to count themselves God-bearers, sent out to share a God too good not to be true. The news fell leaden across the front page: 'Guilty of sexual misconduct with a parishioner'. Blessed fruit turned rotten? Could he ever bring forth Jesus again?

Nothing is too hard for God.

God calls us all in Mary! Her paradigm encounter reveals the method in Divine madness, teaches us to respond to his strange and marvellous ways.

First, we learn, God's call to collaboration is Love's choice, not necessity or obligation. Almighty God can do anything do-able, by simple fiat. So far as task orientation goes, God can do whatever we can do better all by Godself. The sun pulses with light and heat; but the God who said 'Let there be light' (and there was light) could make heat the same way. The God who made Adam from scratch didn't need Mary or Joseph to get another human being. Saints and mystics tell us, face-to-face visions of God dazzle with wonder, flood our emptiness with joy full to bursting. God didn't need Israel to advertise his glory, doesn't require us to spread Good News. Mary's story reveals 'Emmanuel' (God-with-us) as God's favourite name, discloses Divine passion to make the material of our lives his clay, to mould, work them up until they shine like Bethlehem's star!

Second, God always lures us into projects beyond our capacities. Mary had no husband; David no armour; Gideon too few soldiers. Even under normal and optimal conditions, settled in the land with fertile fields and expanding borders, Israel didn't have what it takes to accomplish its heavenly assignment. By definition, nothing we or God can do alone will make Emmanuel, God-with-us. Besides, God's ways are higher than our ways. No matter how hard we try, our appreciation of Divine aims will always be partial and superficial. Yet, this is all right, because God is producer and director, God's the responsibility to keep the show going, to make the plot resolve. We are not called to *make sure* God's purpose succeeds. The performance will not stand or fall with us. But if we give our bit parts all we've got, we can add spice and zest, subtlety, at least humour to the drama!

Third, heavenly husbandry banishes sterility, because nothing is too hard for God! Pushing the century mark, Abraham and Sarah were laughably beyond child-bearing years. But miraculous births and cures were child's play compared to the creativity of Calvary. For God in Christ crucified confronts human degradation the same old Emmanuel way. Christ the victim, crying out in torment, mind blown with bodily pain, guarantees that nothing that happens to us – neither Alzheimer's nor chemical depression, neither MS nor

cancer nor AIDS – can erase God's image in us. Christ
the political prisoner, dying on a garbage dump, proves
that every human person is holy to the Lord, no
matter what cruel tyrants do. Christ dying naked,
sexually abused by passers-by demonstrates that
violation by others can never make us unclean.

Now Emmanuel God loves a challenge. After all,
what is omnipotence for? Our God does not stop with
compensating victims of violence, literally suffering in
and with them, tucking them into the womb in his
side, bearing them up to the Father's right hand. Will
the Creator mimic the creature, by counting serial
killers and child pornographers beyond the pale? Will
God write us off as moral refuse, fake over-achievers
breaking under pressure, destroying ourselves and
others? No! By becoming curse on the cross, God
reaches down to fertilise blasphemy with blessing, not
only to enable us to live with ourselves, but to convert
our worst deeds into positive advance towards something wonderful. Joseph's jealous brothers plotted his
death, sold him into slavery, lied to their old father. But
God turned it to good, to bring life to many.

No matter what we do, God will not let us go until
she blesses us, will not rest until he makes us a blessing
to many. God will make us fruitful willy-nilly. And yet,
like any suitor proposing, God bends all his omniscient
ingenuity to winning our consent. Mary, the disciples
agreed eagerly at the beginning, the future open, full
of wonder and promise, like a newborn child. But
marriage trust, faithfulness are not once and for all, but
daily. The Bible bluntly predicts, we *all* will stumble.
Israel said 'Yes' to betrothal when it killed the paschal

lambs, but was committing adultery with the Golden Calf even while the marriage contract was being chiselled on tablets of stone! And Mother Mary went along with Jesus' brothers who wanted to seize him as a lunatic, get him off the streets. Yet, God wooed them back, helped Israel prepare the Saviour's way, re-plighted Mary's troth with Pentecostal flame.

The Good News is that Mary's, our own perpetual virginity is not a biological fact or zealously guarded spiritual condition. Rather it is sign and seal of God's promise always to begin again, to cover our shame with amazing creativity and joy.

This Advent, Gabriel greets us in Mary, Mary in us: 'Hail, Favoured One! Blessed are you, blessed your fruit! Your fruit is Jesus!' No condition is disqualifying. The Creator knows what he is doing. The offer *is* too good to refuse. Let Mary's lines cue your answer: *'My soul proclaims the greatness of the Lord!'*

[Preached at Christ Church, New Haven, Advent IV, 1993]

TEN

Exiled Blessing

Now after they had left, an angel of the Lord appeared to Joseph in a dream and said, 'Get up, take the child and his mother, and flee to Egypt, and remain there until I tell you; for Herod is about to search for the child, to destroy him.' Then Joseph got up, took the child and his mother by night, and went to Egypt, and remained there until the death of Herod. This was to fulfil what had been spoken by the Lord through the prophet, 'Out of Egypt I have called my son.' . . .

When Herod died, an angel of the Lord suddenly appeared in a dream to Joseph in Egypt and said, 'Get up, take the child and his mother, and go to the land of Israel, for those who were seeking the child's life are dead.' Then Joseph got up, took the child and his mother, and went to the land of Israel. But when he heard that Archelaus was ruling over Judea in place of his father Herod, he was afraid to go there. And after being

warned in a dream, he went away to the district of
Galilee. There he made his home in a town called
Nazareth, so that what had been spoken through the
prophets might be fulfilled, 'He will be called a
Nazorean.' (Matthew 2:13–15, 19–23)

Advent prophesies, Jesse-tree forebears tell, angelic
choirs proclaim blessing without measure, joy overflowing, unending dynasty, health, wealth, security,
happiness unqualified! Today's gospel sobers, pinches
us back to reality, re-minds the unforgettable, how in
this world blessing-bearing is costly; blessing always
mixed.

Blessing sometimes falls down unbidden . . . when
God plucked Abram out of Haran, promised that all
nations would bless themselves through him . . . when
YHWH summoned Moses from the burning bush, called
him from sheepfolds to Pharaoh's court, to 40 years of
wilderness wandering towards promised land . . . when
God called Jeremiah, impregnated Mary with the
Divine Word, made her Mother of God!

Sometimes blessing is elusive, long-desired, begged
for . . . like Isaac, Samuel, late-born sons of barren
mothers . . . like exiles' return from Babylon . . .
like political independence, Hitler's defeat, MIA-
repatriation, rust and crumble Iron Curtain,
end of apartheid . . . like the job of your dreams . . .
like cures for cancer, heart disease, AIDS . . .

Why, sometimes, blessing is even 'stolen' . . . like
trickster Jacob selling Esau red lentils, fooling blind
Isaac with Halloween disguise . . . like holier-than-thou

Pharisees mocking Jesus' disciples . . . like younger brother trying to be cuter when older sister's smarter . . . like colleagues competing for bonuses . . . like developed nations gulping down the world's surplus, buying cheap tee-shirts at the expense of slave labour . . . all ripping off blessing as if there weren't enough to go around!

Any-which-way, blessing is disruptive, crashing through the status quo, threatening not only powers that be, but whole systems of patronage and manipulation. What use is Herod's puppet strut, Sanhedrin's scheming control, when the land flows with milk and honey, when justice rolls down like water, righteousness like an endless stream. Everyone knows how drastic political change brings upheaval, sets everyone jockeying for position. But if Messiah comes, really establishes God's all-inclusive Realm; when scarcity really is a thing of the past, winning and losing at tug-of-turf-wars, all the skills that went with them, will be utterly obsolete.

And here we meet the bitter truth: *most people – we at times – are afraid of blessing, feel we have too much to lose to open ourselves to blessing, to allow it really to come.* Terror is a powerful, violence-provoking motive. Some seize blessing only to toss it away like radioactive waste. Others are watchful, ready to pounce; when they suspect a blessing-bearer move to stamp it, them, out. To do otherwise, requires extraordinary faith in God!

And so, predictably, blessing drives its bearers into exile, to protect the blessing from violent hands . . . Baby Jesus in Egypt . . . Hutu and Tutsi fleeing, chasing murderous machetes . . . battered wives to shelters, with fragments of self-respect . . . misunderstood youth off to college, hitching around the world, escaping alien expectations . . . visions of God's goodness split off, hoarded in deep psychic pockets, out of depression's way, safe from evil's conscious reach . . .

Invariably, given half the chance, blessing makes its bearers immigrant straddlers, resident aliens. Having grown up in one world, they are forced to inhabit another, discover that hot water doesn't have to come out of the left faucet; that salad can be served last; that eyeballs and tongues, even dragonflies, can be eaten; that dress codes and hair cuts come in wild varieties; that gestures are conventional, do not everywhere and always mean the same thing. Exile teaches blessing-bearers spiritual flexibility; loosens their cultural grip, eventually calms fear, awakens imagination: personally, socially, spiritually, good things could be radically different from what we thought, from what they have been, from all they are.

More importantly still, God commanded Abram to leave home, with 40 years of wilderness, God cut Israel off from Egyptian cuisine, carted Judah's ruling classes off to Babylon. With the touch of blessing, God uproots us from ordinary aims and expectations, to proclaim Good News that our God is no mere projection of race or culture, imprisoned in local temples made with human hands, truly worshipped only by 'our kind' of people. No! Our God is Emmanuel, God with us all the time. God blesses us with exile to convince us that we do not live by the sweat of our brow, by the bread of human toil, but by that very Word that proceeds from the mouth of God!

Unsurprisingly, Divine blessing is powerful, possessive, marks us for life. It will never let us return to business as usual. We can try – like Simon Peter – to go back to fishing. We can try to repress it, exile it to basement or attic, with the skeletons in our closet. If we're lucky, we'll succeed about as well as a woman trying to forget she's pregnant. After a while, pretty soon, we'll hear dry bones rattling, knee-bone connecting to thigh-bone, sinew pulling vertebrae into line; we'll feel the kicking and the turning, the expanding pressure until – like Jeremiah – we find ourselves in labour, time to give birth, bring blessing to light!

Since it is too late to back out now, let us pray for courage to capitulate – for Abram's readiness for adventure, Jacob's wily adaptability, Joseph's maturing wisdom; for Sarah's humour, Mary's daring, Magdalene's faithfulness, Paul's confidence and zeal. Let us pray for ears to hear angelic biddings, practise our 'Yes', learn to sing 'Magnificat', pray that our fruit may be Jesus, Emmanuel, the biggest blessing of all!

[Preached at St Thomas', New Haven,
Second Sunday of Christmas, 1997]

ELEVEN

'And immediately . . .'

Now after John was arrested, Jesus came to Galilee, proclaiming the good news of God, and saying, 'The time is
fulfilled, and the kingdom of God has come near; repent,
and believe in the good news.'

   As Jesus passed along the Sea of Galilee, he saw Simon
and his brother Andrew casting a net into the sea – for
they were fishermen. And Jesus said to them, 'Follow me
and I will make you fish for people.' And immediately
they left their nets and followed him. As he went a little
farther, he saw James son of Zebedee and his brother John,
who were in their boat mending the nets. Immediately he
called them; and they left their father Zebedee in the boat
with the hired men, and followed him. They went to
Capernaum; and when the sabbath came, he entered the
synagogue and taught. They were astounded at his teaching, for he taught them as one having authority, and not
as the scribes. (Mark 1:14–20)

St Mark's gospel ushers in God's Reign with startling staccato force. John the Baptist appears Elijah-like, *and immediately* Jesus rises from watery baptismal grave, born again as God's well-beloved Son. *And immediately* the Holy Spirit drives him into the desert to wrestle with demons . . . *And immediately*, Jesus strides into ministry . . . *And immediately* the disciples leave their nets . . . *And immediately* the Messiah invades the synagogue, casts out demons . . . *And immediately* . . . *And immediately* . . . *And immediately* . . .

Make no mistake about it, Mark fires every rhetorical symbol possible: *Now is the time*, when God rends the heavens to come down! *Now is the time*, when the Son of Man descends apocalpytically, shattering everyday worlds. *Now* is the hour of decision, *now time to turn again, now* drop everything, abandon leaky ships and splendid careers, *now (or never?)* follow!

If we were silently awe struck, gently, deeply moved before God-made-vulnerable in a manger, St Mark's demanding approach makes our defences shoot right back up like the Berlin Wall. Rationalisation runs wild. How could Jesus approve, much less require, those fisher brothers to leave their old father in the boat? Besides, abrupt reversals of life commitments, like tent-meeting conversions, are unstable, apt to come unglued as quickly as they were sealed. To bear fruit, a seed needs time to bury itself deep, let its roots network out, infiltrate the heart's every fibre; time to push upward, spread branches, venture leaves, gain nourishment in sunshine, build strength through wind and rain. St Paul seems to be on our side, with his cautious advice to 'grow where you're planted'. How can the gospel thrust run so counter to our very human nature which God himself has made?

This pseudo-problem is an artefact of our otherwise laudable lectionary practice of reading the gospel through in course, roughly one story at a time. Accurate charting of a discipleship career requires us to read the whole book (which incidentally – and yes, this is an advertisement – can be done in a single sitting). Once we take the big picture, and distinguish rhetorical *form* from event-level *content*, we see that God does not begin by blowing the disciples' minds with naked Divinity. No, he comes as a charismatic teacher, delivering a personal invitation to register for a course. With beginning-of-term enthusiasm, students push and shove to sign up, jockey for position. The first half of the syllabus features our favourite miracles, parables and Galilean controversies, and climaxes in the mid-term exam at Caesarea Philippi, when our Lord poses his single, all-or-nothing question: 'Who do you say that I am?' The winking, tongue-in-cheek evangelist lets us know that the disciples are pulling B-/C+, still seeing men as trees walking, confusing Satan's wiles with God's right hand. Despite study retreats, review sessions, they are AWOL for the final exam. And the short ending of Mark's gospel leaves us wondering whether those truants ever managed to make up their incompletes.

In short, we can take heart. Though the Divine course material is guaranteed to be over our heads, God does not expect us to swallow, digest it all like jello, *immediately* in one swift gulp. On the contrary, God shows remarkable patience, resourceful willingness to deal with impossibly slow pupils, who – like us – improve, but never come fully up to speed. In a nutshell, the demands of discipleship are simple; at any given time, at all times and all places, to say 'Yes' as much as we can.

The disciples set a good example, trying with all their might to understand, to get with Jesus' programme. But, like theirs, our 'Yes' will always be filtered through an imperfect conceptual grasp. Their impulse was to silence the competing exorcist who stole the mighty name of 'Jesus' for his own magic spell, like Elijah to call down fire from heaven on the unwelcoming village. On Passion's eve they were still arguing about who was the greatest: even after Pentecost inclined to reserve the Gospel for strictly observant, kosher-keeping Jews. Their preconceptions were peeled away, not immediately, but one by one until eventually they found their worlds turned upside down.

Second, we are called as disciples to trust the teacher enough to voice our questions. Our Lord Jesus himself encourages us to ask, knock, seek, find. Mary isn't bashful with her 'But how can this be?' Patience finally exhausted, Abraham implores, 'How will I know this to be so, when Sarah and I are getting so old?' The gospels are full of disciples' stupid, silly questions. Remember Thomas' plea, 'Lord, we don't know where you are going; how can we know the way?' However embarrassing it was for him to stick his neck out, the Church for centuries has been grateful to know the answer: 'I AM the way, the truth and the life.' And who knows what our queries may yet discover?

Innocent, naive, bungling and confused questions

are one thing. They are raised with a child's humility and curiosity, and we have plenty of them: if God is everywhere, is he in the cereal box? Does God really love cockroaches? Is there life on other planets? If God, well, even the stars and galaxies are so big and we are so small, why does God care at all about human being?

Yet, many of our most important religious questions aren't exploratory, but accusatory. Why do bad things happen to good – at least no worse than average – people? The patriarchs understood God's readiness for candour, stood willing to take their chances in sassing God back! Abraham challenged, 'Shall the judge of the world not do right?' only to discover God's mercy dancing out ahead. Moses contended with God not to abandon Israel over the Golden Calf incident, only to find himself conned into more leadership commitment than before. Crying out in agony, Job called God more chaos monster than Creator. Surprisingly, angry hostile questions not only draw a scold, require an apology, but win the reward of face-to-face intimacy with God.

Like most students, we don't always do our home-work. And we pay for it later with diminished ability to say 'Yes'. The disciples couldn't exorcise epilepsy, didn't have enough strength for Gethsemane's trial, because they slept through their prayer life. Like children pretending to be grown-ups, they had bluffed it, not been out in the open with Jesus about their fears. Yet, how often have we wept through the night, crying out to God with tears of terror, only to find ourselves strong to face Goliath in the morning. Refusing to admit resentment at the harsh demanding God made in their own image, Pharisees and Sadducees wrenched matters into their own hands, shrunk Messianic hopes down to human-sized, ethnic preservation.

Imagine Peter's remorse, humiliation . . . someone who said 'Yes' as much as he could, only to find there wasn't enough to him to be loyal where it counts. Imagine Judas, who threw himself into a cause, only in his confusion to feel cut out, betrayed by it . . . who, betraying in return, shredded his integrity, dismembered his soul before killing the body. The deep truth about us is that we are all morally flimsy, covertly willing to sell out at some terrible price. Does this mean we flunk the course without the possibility of a rewrite?

Not according to our baptismal vows! God doesn't call us to be heroes with stamina to do it by ourselves, but saints, who – however much we fall and hurt – turn again, crawl back up into mommy's lap *immediately*. God our Creator is our Re-Creator, healing, repairing, confronting, consoling, forgiving, sending us out with his power to strengthen one another, right now, *immediately*!

[Preached at Christ Church, New Haven,
Epiphany III, 1994]

TWELVE

'Beloved, love one another; for love is of God'

Beloved, let us love one another, because love is from God; everyone who loves is born of God and knows God. Whoever does not love does not know God, for God is love. God's love was revealed among us in this way: God sent his only Son into the world so that we might live through him. In this is love, not that we loved God but that he loved us and sent his Son to be the atoning sacrifice for our sins. Beloved, since God loved us so much, we also ought to love one another. No one has ever seen God; if we love one another, God lives in us, and his love is perfected in us.

By this we know that we abide in him and he in us, because he has given us of his Spirit. And we have seen and do testify that the Father has sent his Son as the Saviour of the world. God abides in those who confess that Jesus is the Son of God, and they abide in God. So we have known and believe the love that God has for us.

'Beloved, love one another; for love is of God'

God is love, and those who abide in love abide in God, and God abides in them. Love has been perfected among us in this: that we may have boldness on the day of judgement, because as he is, so are we in this world. There is no fear in love, but perfect love casts out fear; for fear has to do with punishment, and whoever fears has not reached perfection in love. We love because he first loved us. Those who say, 'I love God,' and hate their brothers or sisters, are liars; for those who do not love a brother or sister whom they have seen, cannot love God whom they have not seen. The commandment we have from him is this: those who love God must love their brothers and sisters also.

(1 John 4:7–21)

'As the Father has loved me, so I have loved you; abide in my love. If you keep my commandments, you will abide in my love, just as I have kept my Father's commandments and abide in his love. I have said these things to you so that my joy may be in you, and that your joy may be complete.

'This is my commandment, that you love one another as I have loved you. No one has greater love than this, to lay down one's life for one's friends. You are my friends if you do what I command you. I do not call you servants any longer, because the servant does not know what the master is doing; but I have called you friends, because I have made known to you everything that I have heard from my Father. You did not choose me but I chose you. And I appointed you to go and bear fruit, fruit that will last, so that the Father will give you whatever you ask him in my name. I am giving you these commands so that you may love one another.' (John 15:9–17)

Today's lectionary gives the preacher scarcely any room to manoeuvre. It virtually forces us to focus on that four-letter word *'love'*! You might wonder why I should mind, why I should number 'love' with other terms that shouldn't be mentioned in church. My reason is that 'love' has become a weasel word in our society, as apt to seduce and mislead as to edify and inspire.

On the one hand, we tend to *sentimentalise* it. Love is warm fuzzies, with emotionally one-dimensional cupids flanking the sides of a Hallmark card or a choco-late candy heart. On this rendering, to be loving means making people feel good, requires us to take responsi-bility for their feelings, which translates into putting ourselves at their manipulative disposal. Or else it means feeling good about others – which of course we don't always. So either we feel guilty or we get into a cycle of repression.

Our culture's injunction to love sentimentally sets up a no-win situation, because feelings aren't within our direct voluntary control. I can't control how I feel, much less how you feel. At a deeper level, it invites us to lie about human life and human nature: we shouldn't feel good about everything we experience. For feelings are one way of monitoring our environ-ment, and many circumstances are manifestly dangerous to our health! One thing is sure, our Lord Jesus Christ wasn't feeling good about life, and those who murdered him, while he was dying on the cross!

Alternatively, we *romanticise* love. Secular culture does this by *sexualising* it. In popular songs, lovers begin with the idolatrous pretense that they can be everything to each other: 'I can't live without you.' 'You are my sunshine; you are my rain.' 'I will take care of you, be your only one.' Before the tune is over, though, these promises are translated into the demand that the partner satisfy the other's sexual needs. Movies and commercials bombard us with the same message: to become worthy of love, you need to use our pro-duct to become sexually attractive.

Contrary to St Augustine's reputation, the Christian religion is not against sex. But it does oppose this caricature of love on every count. For love requires us to meet, first and foremost, as persons. Human sexuality is misused whenever biology is divorced from the social context of personal intimacy. For Christians, sexual expression is demoted from the centre, to one dimension of some personal relationships.

More importantly, it is a lie that any one person can be everything to another. Even in the blessed Trinity, the Father needs both Son and Holy Spirit, the Holy Spirit both Son and Father, the Son both Father and Holy Spirit – even each Divine person needs at least two others to be fully itself!

Both of these distortions – love-as-good-feeling and love-as-biological – respond to our deep need to believe that loving one another is really possible by covering up the hard fact: that all but the most super-ficial human relationships involve conflicts; the more personally intimate they are, the deeper the issues become. Love-as-feeling, promoted by the greeting card industry, invites us to create a temporary illusion by whipping up good feelings at Thanksgiving, Christmas and Mother's Day. Love-as-sex encourages us to substitute biological contact for the real thing; after all, people can 'do it' even if they don't know each other . . . some marriages prove, even if they hate each other. The trouble is that family holidays often erupt into fights; 'loving' and leaving produces terrible wounds; and in any event there is the morning after, when we feel lonelier than ever.

Curiously, we Christians combine the first of these fakeries with the opposite extreme. After all, we are disciples of a Lord whose ministry was dedicated to exposing conflict. The central symbol of our religion is an instrument of torture. Did he not say 'Turn the other cheek. Walk the second mile. Take up your cross daily . . .'? Focusing on these sayings, we romanticise *love-as-martyrdom*, conceive of our calling as making ourselves the ready-willing-and-able targets of other's abuse. Surely if we allow others to keep acting out on us, while we smile sweetly, meek as lambs, they will eventually wake up and repent; and *we* will have shared with Christ in their redemption!

But this, too, is a travesty of what our Lord Jesus was about. Our Lord did allow himself to be crucified. His violent end was provoked by a prophetic determination to bring God's judgement, by calling a spade a spade, confronting people with harsh truths that they didn't want to hear.

Truth is also a standard of our Christian love for one another. More precisely, our interactions must meet the test of not defacing but evoking the image of Christ in the other person. Abuse tells the lie that the abusers cannot be who they were created to be without destroying what God created someone else to be.

Authoritarian relationships tell the lie that one cannot be as big as he needs to be in Christ without the other being smaller that she really is. Saviour complexes tell the lie that one cannot fulfil herself unless the other remains permanently in need of her rescue. Christ's love command requires us to step out of, to contradict by word and action, any such neurotic dramas in which we may be involved. But this is not the same as 'making' the other person recognise what she is doing. Nor is it a general license to speak the truth about what we see wrong with another person, whether or not we have been invited into that level of intimacy. Making sure everyone faces the truth and gets saved is Christ's vocation, not ours.

My point is that to love one another is the general vocation of all Christians. But the precise shape that love takes is also a matter of particular vocation. Unlike God, we have a finite capacity for personal intimacy. We cannot even meet, much less personally interact with, every person in the world. If we tried, we would spread ourselves too thin and end by not loving anyone. In the universal drama of redemption, we will have to work hard at our bit parts, loving the particular people God calls us to love in the way God invites us to love them. That will be the most we are capable of.

What about loving one another where we live and work and pray? I think we do well to begin with respect and its several-fold manifestations. First, in the context of our parish family, *we can pay each other the compliment of real attention.* Believe me, people in our society are starved for it. Most all of us are capable of listening attentively to someone else for five minutes each Sunday. The conversations do not have to be deeply self-revealing, much less problem-solving, to have the effect of acknowledging the other's dignity as a person, not a thing. Believe me again: five minutes can make all the difference!

Second, *we can love by not caricaturing one another.* Each of us suffers from the fallen-human tendency to oversimplify and cubby-hole other people. But we can catch ourselves in the act, repent and ask God to correct our vision. As a priest I have learned that behind every face is a struggle, courage to persevere, and a unique point of view that deserves nuanced understanding.

Corollary to this, *we can refuse to gossip about one another.* This doesn't mean pretending that we don't have faults. Each of us is a sinner. But there is a difference between recognising a truth and seeking to blind others to the image of Christ in another person. And we can and should beware.

Fourth, *we can try to get to know at least some other persons in the parish better.* They may be the people we meet in class, in choir, on committees, or workdays, or simply the ones who typically sit in our pew. None of us will find everyone equally easy to relate to. But each of us can take small risks, reach out to someone. After all, we have our Lord Jesus in common. And his yoked pairings are often surprising.

Finally, *we can pray for our parish family in general, and we can make it a point to pray for at least some individuals in particular.* Prayer links us together even without direct communication or intimate conversation, at levels too deep for words. After all, the Holy

Spirit is the spirit of prayer, and hers is the tie that binds our hearts in Christian love.

These steps may seem a far cry from St John's lofty words, 'Love one another.' Certainly, they are a far cry from the way God loves. Nevertheless, I commend them because they are real steps, not quackery. And they can be the beginning of true love.

[Preached at St Augustine's-by-the-Sea, Easter VI, 1991]

THIRTEEN

Fraudulent Forgiveness

Then Peter came and said to him, 'Lord, if another member of the church sins against me, how often should I forgive? As many as seven times?' Jesus said to him, 'Not seven times, but, I tell you, seventy-seven times.

'For this reason the kingdom of heaven may be compared to a king who wished to settle accounts with his slaves. When he began the reckoning, one who owed him ten thousand talents was brought to him; and, as he could not pay, his lord ordered him to be sold, together with his wife and children and all his possessions, and payment to be made. So the slave fell on his knees before him, saying, "Have patience with me, and I will pay you everything." And out of pity for him, the lord of that slave released him and forgave him the debt. But that same slave, as he went out, came upon one of his fellow slaves who owed him a hundred denarii; and seizing him by the throat, he said, "Pay what you owe." Then his fellow slave fell down and

pleaded with him, "Have patience with me, and I will pay you." But he refused; then he went and threw him into prison until he would pay the debt. When his fellow slaves saw what had happened, they were greatly distressed, and they went and reported to their lord all that had taken place. Then his lord summoned him and said to him, "You wicked slave! I forgave you all that debt because you pleaded with me. Should you not have had mercy on your fellow slave, as I had mercy on you?" And in anger his lord handed him over to be tortured until he would pay his entire debt. So my heavenly Father will also do to every one of you, if you do not forgive your brother or sister from your heart.' (Matthew 18:21–35)

Do I *have* to forgive him? When I joined the company, he was so helpful, giving me the lowdown, everything from past project performance to office politics. We lunched together every day. I was really open with him, brainstormed out loud. Then he took my best idea to the boss, represented it as his own, got the big promotion, started spreading innuendos about me. Every-body thinks he's above reproach. There's nothing I can do but look for another job. 'Do I *have* to forgive him?' 'Seventy times seven!'

'True, I wasn't there for her. How could I be, commuting back and forth to New York every day, trying to make a living, pay for the suburban house, two cars and the dog, private schools. I was glad for her not to work, to devote herself to the kids. But when I found out she was cheating on me, everything turned to ashes. 'Do I *have* to forgive her?' 'Seventy times seven!'

Her voice was low, her eyes desperate. 'All through high school, my father got up in the middle of the night, entered my room, violated me. For years, I have been emotionally at sea, now crashing under tidal-wave depressions, now riding a surf of guilt. At last, I'm angry at the right person! 'Do I *have* to forgive him?' 'Seventy times seven!'

Forgiveness! What could be more characteristic of our Lord's teaching than the forgiveness of sins? And yet, as a pastor and teacher, I have to confess how often the Church perverts good news of the forgiveness of sins into the demand for pious fraud. What is more, the Bible puts us up to it, and nowhere more emphatically than in the gospel according to Matthew!

We all know, we have learned the dynamic from mother's knee. Someone offends you – not just a little thing like bumping you in the crowd, stepping on your toe – but insult, injustice, betrayal of serious proportions. Anger wells up, the desire to strike back, get even, at least protest. Christian conscience warns with Matthew's words – 'Turn the other cheek! Walk the second mile!' 'Love, pray for your enemies!' It reinforces admonition with threats – 'God won't forgive you if you don't forgive others!' 'Anger is sinful, makes you unfit for polite society,' 'up to your room'; where God is involved, anger excommunicates, casts you into outer darkness, into that lake of fire prepared for the devil and all his angels. As Freud would say, the Christian superego works time and a half, especially on Sundays! Such dire consequences demand a 'quick fix'. So, naturally, we straighten up, smile sweetly, return the soft answer, try to convince all and sundry – God and the adults especially – that we really are good Christian boys and girls.

'Quick fix' is a pious fraud because it doesn't work. When someone does us wrong, feelings of anger and pain testify that it ought not to be so. But we can't afford to dwell on that fact if we're supposed to get over it on the spot. So we cast our true feelings into outer darkness, bury them in psychic basements. For better and worse, out of sight does not mean gone for good. Repression sets up a war in our members: the more we deny on the surface, the more we unconsciously affirm, the more anger and resentment collects in wells down below, depending on our temperament, to seep out in chronic complaints or double-edged barbed remarks, or one day to erupt geyser-like splattering destruction all around. 'Quick fix' is a pious fraud, because it turns us into 'whitewashed sepulchres', can't enable us to forgive from the heart.

Truth to tell, 'quick fix' doesn't enable us to forgive *at all*, because it pressures us to pretend that we really haven't been offended, urges us to believe the other person wasn't himself, under the circumstances couldn't help it, didn't really mean any harm. 'Quick fix' calls on us to *excuse* the offender, *condone* her deed, *acquiesce* in such treatment as we have received. Etymology to the contrary, real forgiveness doesn't cover up but *confronts* the fact of genuine offence, of responsible agency. Real forgiveness acknowledges that they did us wrong on purpose, with their eyes open; enters into, savours just how bad it was; only then refuses to exact an eye for an eye; lets go of hatred and resentment; foregoes revenge.

Nor do 'quick-fix' lies end there. 'Quick fix' is a pious fraud because it blames the victim: if we were not wronged, then we must be, have done, something to deserve it; the universe must be so arranged that it was all right for others to treat us this way – for the spouse to beat, the boss to exploit, co-workers to take advantage of us.

'Quick fix' is a pious fraud because it places us in spiritual jeopardy. Not only do we have to absorb the injury; we have either to find some toxic waste disposal for our pain and anger, or stain ourselves with the guilt of unforgiveness. All of which makes 'quick fix' a blasphemous fraud, because it tempts us to sin, to despair of God's will and power to heal, of Divine intention to seek and save the lost!

Matthew is hard-sell on this subject. But when you stop to think about it, today's parable seems to rest on a false analogy. God is the ideal patron-king; we are the clients. Patron-kings are wealthy; generosity befits their station, advertises their resources to be so vast that the client's debt is nothing to them. By contrast, clients are poor; so far from operating with a surplus, their plight would be desperate, they would perish without the patron's aid. Left to themselves, one client cannot afford to absorb the loss when a fellow client defaults. The reason we can't easily forgive is that we are radically vulnerable, capable of giving and receiving wounds that wreck us beyond our capacity to repair. So how can God expect, how could we ever be in a position to respond, seventy times seven?

Maybe we could, if we were so sure of heavenly patronage that we felt we could count God's wealth as our own. But today's story with its final scene of Divine reversal and retribution undercuts such confidence, refuses to encourage in order to warn.

Happily, the Bible offers many images, for different rhetorical purposes and moods. Flipping back to the beginning of the chapter, we find Jesus comparing the kingdom of heaven to nursery school, whose enrolment is restricted to little children. The playground is rough and tumble, full of skinned knees and squabbles. Sometimes we call each other names; other times, we haul off and slug each other until it hurts really bad.

For God's human children, forgiveness is no 'quick fix' but a seventy-times-seven process based on consolation and comfort. It begins by running to Mother Jesus, crawling up on his lap, thrashing, crying, accusing with childlike candour and abandon; carrying on until our energy is spent; snuggling up, catching our breath, carrying on some more, pouring out pain and rage again and again, seventy times seven until the wells are drained.

Like good mothers everywhere, Jesus knows how to take our outcries seriously – he knows how much it hurts; he suffered, too – without crediting our accusations at face value. Our Creator knows how human feelings caricature, demonise what seems to threaten at the core.

Mother Jesus gives birth to our change of heart, not by arguing with our premises, but by making us feel safe, by showing us his surplus – love in abundance, more than we could ask or imagine, life eternal. Returning to his lap, seventy times seven, as often as it takes, convinces us of our connection, her strength;

elicits the boast that our Lord and Mother Jesus is so resourceful, he can make good on anything!

And so, unsurprisingly, our Lord and Mother Jesus knew what he was talking about. Seventy-times-seven forgiveness is a *must* because it heals, unbinds energy trapped in caverns of bitterness and rage, thaws frozen defences, brightens our confidence that we are deeply valued, frees us to entrust everybody to Mother Jesus, and run off to play!

[Preached at St Thomas', New Haven,
Pentecost Season, 1996]

PART THREE

Whose Purity?

FOURTEEN

Squeaky Clean

In those days Mary set out and went with haste to a Judean town in the hill country, where she entered the house of Zechariah and greeted Elizabeth. When Elizabeth heard Mary's greeting, the child leaped in her womb. And Elizabeth was filled with the Holy Spirit and exclaimed with a loud cry, 'Blessed are you among women, and blessed is the fruit of your womb. And why has this happened to me, that the mother of my Lord comes to me? For as soon as I heard the sound of your greeting, the child in my womb leaped for joy. And blessed is she who believed that there would be a fulfilment of what was spoken to her by the Lord.' And Mary said,

> *'My soul magnifies the Lord,*
> *and my spirit rejoices in God my Saviour,*
> *for he has looked with favour on the lowliness of his*
> *servant.*

*Surely, from now on all generations will call me
    blessed;*
*for the Mighty One has done great things for me,
    and holy is his name.*
*His mercy is for those who fear him
    from generation to generation.*
*He has shown strength with his arm;
    he has scattered the proud in the thoughts of their
    hearts.*
*He has brought down the powerful from their thrones,
    and lifted up the lowly;*
*he has filled the hungry with good things,
    and sent the rich away empty.*
*He has helped his servant Israel,
    in remembrance of his mercy,*
*according to the promise he made to our ancestors,
    to Abraham and to his descendants forever.'*
*And Mary remained with her about three months
and then returned to her home.* (Luke 1:39–56)

Immaculate . . . her house was immaculate . . . furniture polished to pass the white-glove test . . . invisible windows . . . gleaming floors . . . a place for everything and everything in its place . . . *until* the seven-year-old tramped in with muddy feet, knocked over the ketchup bottle on the fresh linen table cloth, sending the glass of chocolate milk crashing to the floor.

Such episodes teach us that dirt is stuff out of order; that clean is fragile and dirty is catching; that dirt spreads by contact; mussy touching is the thing to avoid.

Such fundamentals account for a good deal of family friction. Perhaps for that reason they get used to interpret our relationship to God. Didn't we learn that sin stains because it puts us out of order . . . because holy and unholy don't mix, makes us unfit to come into the presence of God? Stubborn stains call for a total cleanser of wonder-working power. Yet, water from the side of Christ, blood pulsing from his wounds can't cleanse unless Christ is pure himself. And that's a problem. How could Christ be clean in his human nature and still be a member of our messed-up family, a son of Adam's race?

Duns Scotus championed the solution that Mary the Mother of God must herself have been immaculately conceived – born and preserved forever free of those tendencies to sin against which we daily struggle. A pure mother will not contaminate the child within her. He will burst into this world, with birth pangs, through water and blood, spotless and undefiled.

I can hear your protest coming: 'You mean, they pay theologians good money to think up things like that! Anyone can see, this calculation from the logic of dirt and cleanness is full of holes!' For one thing, we can press our question back a stage: what about St Anne, Mary's mother? What about grandma and great grandma? If clean babies can only come from clean mothers, God had better take his miracle bath all the way back to Eve! On the other hand, if God is going to do it supernaturally, why get the mothers involved? God could protect Baby Jesus with an invisible shield, so that he doesn't 'catch' original sin the usual way. Again, everybody knows, pure water cleanses by becoming dirty itself. If Jesus is going to wash away our sins, how can he stay pure in the process? Besides, isn't Jesus supposed to be God with us? Didn't God become human so that he could share our struggles and frustrations, our pain and grief? How could Christ be 'tempted in all things as we are' if he had a sinless mother?

How easily the transparent becomes muddy! All of which shows us our need to think and think again.

Go back to the intuition that dirt is stuff out of order, to our housekeeping ideal of a place for everything and everything in its place. Leviticus insists that God must be meticulous, like an effective mother, requires our strict co-operation to keep things rigidly organised in the household of God. We should no more mix kinds – linsy woolsy, polycotton, mules and capons – than put forks where knives belong or laundry detergent on the cereal shelf. When we spill out of our natural boundaries with runny noses and bleeding sores, we need a ritual bath to make us fit for polite society. Vigilance is required to keep bugs out of cooking pots on penalty of throwing them away or burying them in the ground. In Levitical mouths, 'You must be holy because I am holy' turns into a Divine threat of banishment: 'Neaten up, or get thrown out!'

Yet, with Mary, we might ask those priestly authors, 'How can this be?' Look all around you. The world is a mess. Surely the Cosmic Housekeeper has not created a place for everything, kept everything in its place! On the contrary, God seems more like most of us who get our homes just a little more organised than necessary for daily functioning. The laundry gets done with the weekly mystery of disappearing socks, food is generally in the pantry but we forgot the orange juice, and where did we put the cookie press or holiday bow tie or that jewellery we hid while on vacation? And nowadays there is the accumulating pile of recyclables that conscience won't let us throw away!

Genesis 1 begins to spill the family secret. God did fit most animals into natural places – sheep to land, trout to water, eagles to sky – define ways of moving around, design limbs appropriate to each. But what about shrimp and lobsters, water animals without fins and scales? Snakes squirming over land with no legs? Swarming insects with their unruly navigation? Worst of all, pigs, mammals who part the hoof but don't chew the cud? Genesis pronounces such animals are 'unclean', 'out of order' because they don't fit the categories. Moreover, God took no pains to make boundary-blurring hybrids impossible – like putting clothes in piles without any dividers in the drawer. Doesn't Saint Paul say that God grafts wild olive branches to the domesticated tree; moves Gentiles out of the ghetto into respectable Jewish neighbourhoods?

To wash the family linen in public, our God loves variety, is an irrepressible mixer of kinds. To put it bluntly, our God just can't stand to keep in his place, confined like an Oriental potentate to a heavenly throne with CIA agents dispatched to wander to and fro and report back to headquarters. No, our God loves the world so much that he had to become part of it, enter creation at its centre, where kinds mix most, in human being where spirit enlivens matter and matter chafes against spirit. Our God simply insists on becoming one of us.

The basic problem about incarnation is not how to take an untainted human nature out of Adam's fallen race, but how to put infinite and eternal, almighty fountainhead of wisdom and goodness, together with something so teensy-weensy, so temporary and flimsy as human being. But our God loves a challenge, scoffs at racial differences, delights in cross-fertilisation. So far from a meticulous housekeeper, our God is a relentless lover who will stop at nothing to unite his beloved to himself.

Like a love-struck suitor, God embraced our poverty, rumoured illegitimacy, the pain of desertion and betrayal, the shame of tortured crucifixion, even Death and the grave; he hugged them tight to himself, because he is Emmanuel and they are our lot. God stretched out his arms on the hard wood of the cross, stained himself with blasphemy and curse, became ritually unclean to assure us that nothing – not even the most horrendous things we have done to self or others – can make us so filthy as to separate us from his love! God in Christ Jesus, high and lifted up, echoes that Levitical cry: 'You must be holy because I am holy!'

How can this be? Because the calculus of purity and defilement got one axiom wrong. For in God's hands, cleanness is not fragile, but dirt vanishes at the touch of a holy God. Our God is holy and our God is every-where. No matter what we suffer, no matter what mud puddles we have splashed in, whatever defilement we have embraced, God has run out ahead to greet us: 'I can, I will, I have already made you clean.'

This Advent the Good News is that we are all immaculately conceived children of a holy God. Mother Mary is our song. Mary is immaculate because God-with-us is immaculate. She catches it from him. And we, born through the birth pangs of the cross, washed by water and the blood of Jesus, are also clean by contact. We are all full of grace, heirs of great promise, destined for eternal fruitfulness. And for this we give thanks and praise to God!

[Preached at St Mary's, Palms, Immaculate Conception of the Blessed Virgin Mary, 1994]

FIFTEEN

Queer Variety

Our God loves variety. My medieval friends thought it was metaphysically predictable that this should be so. They understood God to be an infinite ocean of Goodness. Taking a page from pseudo-Dionysius, they insisted that Goodness by its very nature was disposed to share itself. But because God is so very, very big and every created nature is so very, very small, no single creaturely way of being could possibly exhaust the riches of Deity. Rather God makes myriads of kinds each reflecting who God is from a different angle. What else could explain giraffes and kangaroos, platypus and penguins? Nothing could be anything without expressing something of Divine glory. Together, the whole zoo of kinds is able to make a significant statement about who God is. Taking issue with Origen, my medieval friends insisted, a homogenised cosmos – say one containing only disembodied spirits – would have a lot less to say!

God's ways are not our ways. The Bible and experience tell us so. This, too, was metaphysically predictable. God is very, very big and we are very, very small. We are not smart enough to see as God sees. Our attention span is not wide enough to keep all that detail in mind. Moreover, we cannot dwell in chaos. Sanity requires us to get things organised, conceptually speaking. That's why we imagine God created by separating and defining and drawing sharp boundaries. We oversimplify the variety of creation so that we can have a map to negotiate the world by. God must be willing to work with these limitations. After all, God is all wise and all knowing. If God had wanted something different, God would have made something else.

Still, this puts God and us in something of a bind. For God is a God of Truth. And God created us to grow in the knowledge and love of God and of one another. Oversimplifications may get enough right to seem useful. But they also impoverish and caricature, worse yet devalue and depreciate the world that surrounds. We set up our cubby holes as normative. What doesn't fit them with precision is unclean, defective, thrust to the margins, cast into outer darkness with weeping and teeth-gnashing. The Holiness Code joins the newspapers and our own experience in telling us so. We are not smart enough to see as God sees. God must be willing to work with these limitations. But God can't be true to Godself and to the wonders of creation if God simply tolerates them. We can't be true to ourselves, express as much about God as we can, without stretching beyond our way of looking at things, our

123

ways of loving things. And we can't be true to each other either.

Now God *is* Truth and our only true Teacher. God knows we are limited developmental creatures. And God must be willing to work with us. Once again, if God had wanted something different, God would have made something else. Divine pedagogy starts where we are with our grids and social constructions, but challenges us with contradictory evidence, allows it to mount up until we can't stand the dissonance, until we have to let our worlds go to smash and start all over again. God has a problem. Our world-views are inspired by reality but wildly out of focus. Queerness is one solution: to call individuals who evoke our categories but also caricature and contradict them; to put front and centre individuals who – by straddling and blurring boundaries – call us beyond our cartoon worlds into the deeper realities of ourselves, of others and of God.

The synoptic gospels press the question, who is Jesus? All three show us, *Jesus Christ is queer.* All three toss up a welter of traditional theological titles and rubrics – rabbi, prophet, S/son of M/man, son of David, King of the Jews, King of Israel, the One who comes in the name of the Lord, Suffering Servant, the Christ, the Son of the living God. Jesus squeezes under only to misfit, overlap, superimpose, contradict each and all of them, because the reality of Jesus is so much more than any of them can say. And this isn't merely because Jesus is God (although my medieval friends certainly don't lose sight of how queer that is). Human personality itself is unique and inexhaustibly mysterious. The synoptic gospels give us a Jesus who strides through Galilee, up and down the countryside, on towards Jerusalem, reversing norms, welcoming the queer, the misfits and outcasts, as vanguards of God's real world order. You say 'leper' but I say 'clean'; you say 'bleeding woman' but I say 'faith making whole'; you say 'traitor', 'tax-collector', 'sinner', but I say 'disciple'. Sometimes Jesus only winks with parables and aphorisms – 'only the sick need a doctor', 'they love much who have been forgiven much', don't you know? Other times Jesus is downright confrontational: you say 'holier than thou', but I say 'hypocrites', 'brood of vipers', 'whitewashed tombs,' narrow-mindedness killing creativity, withering limbs, blinding eyes, amputating instincts, whittling you into a monstrous fragment of your real selves!

Because our God loves variety, God created, calls each of us to live into our queerness. But human need to nail things down and get things organised turns queer discipleship into a tricky task. How quickly political correctness domesticates, takes the teeth out of disturbing testimony. We push and shove our way under the rubric of valorising diversity. 'Dialoguing our differences' becomes a cliché. 'Gay', 'lesbian', 'straight', 'bisexual', 'transgendered' are installed as newly ossified categories. Andrew Sullivan, in his book *Virtually Normal*, tells how after being 'out' for a while, he woke up to the fact that he was still role-playing, this time trying to live into counter-cultural conventions about what it is to be gay. I know others who scramble to live into Sullivan's title, to be virtual-ly normal. As a 1960s' anti-war protester, a childless married woman who's barged her way into two or three male professions, who's misfitted every category ever offered to her, I get impatient with this. *'Why be virtually normal, when you could be interesting?'* I want to say.

I know from experience, this question has sobering answers. Authentic queerness involves blood, sweat and tears, Gethsemane wrestlings through self-doubts and self-loathing, the perils of insecure and costly discernment. There's a thin line – how can I tell the difference? – between creative and crazy, between being an 'original' like Jesus and being demonic or perverse? It took Jesus the proverbial forty days, his disciples a post-resurrection fifty to get the hang of it. External signals are not infallible. Remember Matthew Shepherd? Remember Martin Luther King? Jesus' enemies never 'got' it. He died on a cross!

Divinity School is a crucible where – if all goes well – identities melt down by sometime in the second year, and emerge at graduation in a state of semi-solid reform. To make the most of our time here, we will need to be intentional about three things. First, to help one another to become authentically queer, we'll need to establish some *taboo-free zones* – whether centres, coalitions, prayer groups, supper clubs – communities of understanding, trust and candour, where we can try things on for size and receive honest feedback about how they fit. We'll need lots of these, because culture and experience grip us with different fears and build in contrasting tolerances. None of us can really be there for just anyone else. Second, to learn to use our queerness to herald the Gospel, we'll need practice in 'coming out' to some who are sincerely convinced we are drastically wrong. Sparks may fly, Gethsemanes may multiply. But we'll all be spiritually the deeper for it if we can pray our way together through hell and high water, right down to the Ground of Being, to experience how we're each and all rooted and grounded there.

Our God loves variety. Queerness is not just about gender and sexual orientation. It's about refusing to be a copy of a copy, a slogan, or a cliché. Queerness can be fun. Queerness can be rowdy. Queerness will certainly cost you. But it's a way to be like Jesus, our way to become commercials for a God who is very, very big, even though we are very, very small!

[All School Conference/Gay, Lesbian, Straight, Bisexual Coalition, Niebuhr Hall, 2002]

SIXTEEN

Blessed Holy Family!

Isaiah 62:6–7, 10–12; Titus 3:4–7; Luke 2:15–20

Towards the end of Rite II's Eucharistic Prayer B, the celebrant is invited to 'fill in the blank' with his/her choice of saints whom we hope to join in glory. Most priests supply 'the Blessed Virgin Mary' along with the patron of the house and the commemoree of the day or week. One early morning at Berkeley Divinity School, a colleague of mine startled us out of this routine with 'Blessed Holy Family'. Coming from her, this simple insertion was a homily of several points.

Herself a married mother of children, she was giving voice to Reformation protests against early church and medieval asceticism, against the cult of virginity, which made sexually active married couples second-class citizens in the kingdom of heaven. Implicitly, she was agreeing with sixties-onward pop psychology that repression is a bad thing. She was transposing this into the theological recognition that heterosexuality is a gift of God, fertility a Divine blessing: 'Be fruitful and multiply and replenish the earth!' Gesturing towards the religious right, she was also staking her claim for 'family values', reaching back to that fifties ideology that God intended humans to live in nuclear families with father and mother, 2.5 kids, and a dog. Other 'Christian right' resonances – of patriarchal structure, where parents *rule* children and 'father knows best' – she may or may not have intended. After all, she was a professional woman and not a stay-at-home mom.

Blessed Holy Family! There is much to welcome in this theme. How tender the Genesis 2:23 reassurance, that God created a companion and helpmate for Adam whose inventory of the other animals didn't discover anything 'like enough to himself'! How encouraging that our Lord Jesus echoes YHWH's blessing on marriage where partners leave parents to cling to their spouse! How startling that prophets style YHWH as Israel's husband, how profound the mystery that Ephesians can speak of a mystical marriage between Christ and his Church!

Here at Christ Church, we have couples who show us how the family can be the grammar school of love, who have dared the for-better-and-worse experiment for decades, who – despite mutual flaws and imperfections, unexpected difficulties and dysfunctional dynamics – have muddled through, made mid-course corrections, actually enabled one another to grow in the capacity to love; who – in one way and another, despite mistakes, hurts, misunderstandings, even alienation – have fostered in their children the strength to embrace challenges with creativity. We have only to open our eyes to see in our own members how tenacity can give love quality and texture that even in seniority can house surprises. Most of us have known, maybe a few of us have been, persons who grew up in happy families, who learned to love by being loved first, and so could readily embrace disciplines that freed them to attend to other people and other things. Who can deny, who should not thank God for truly happy families, for the social stability, personal nurture and spiritual opportunities they provide!

All the same, it is idolatrous, to conflate 'Blessed Holy Family' with some fusion of 'religious right', 'Ozzie-and-Harriet' 'family values'. Ozzie and Harriet were supposed to represent a *happy* fifties family, that could take the bitter with the sweet but still grow in commitment, wisdom and love. Significantly, it wasn't a family in which father and sons went off to war and returned dead or disabled. It wasn't a family with schizophrenia, Down's syndrome, or chronic depression, where someone was afflicted with muscular dystrophy or brain cancer or AIDS. It wasn't a family in which marriage partners were unfaithful to each other, or whose children got arrested for trafficking in drugs. We have to ask, *does a family have to be a happy family to be a holy family?*

Again, elementary social anthropology will tell you that family structures have differed widely across time and place, that the nuclear family is a recent cultural artefact, that 'marriage' in the Bible refers to sharply contrasting institutions, from the polygamy of the patriarchs to the quickie divorces of Palestinian Judaism to the mutual consent agreements of Roman law. How then can it be – as the religious right insists – that it is the population of the family – the heterosexual couple with 2.5 kids and a dog – and the roles defining the divisions of power and labour that make a family holy, when even in the Bible these change over its roughly 1800-year time span?

Blessed Holy Family! Clearly, the gospels do not portray JMJ – Jesus, Mary and Joseph – as an Ozzie-and-Harriet family settled in the American suburbs behind their white picket fence! Matthew and Luke make a big point of telling us, Joseph was *not* the father of Mary's child. John's gospel hints, Jesus' earthly career was haunted by the spectre of illegitimacy. Matthew emphasises how *Pax Romana* licensed local tyranny, how Jesus' birth occasioned a slaughter of innocents as in Rwanda and former Yugoslavia, how JMJ numbered themselves among the refugees, geographically uprooted, not once but twice. The synoptic gospels imply that by the time Jesus reached adulthood, Mary was widowed, economically dependent on her male children. Yet, Jesus refused to play the dutiful stay-at-home elder brother, insisted that he must be about his heavenly Father's business, became a wandering teacher, opened himself to the charge of being a drunkard and a glutton, a good for nothing who dishonours his parents, worthy of stoning according to Jewish Law. Not only did Jesus 'divorce', cut flesh-and-blood ties with, his family of origin, he did not marry or father children either. Like Jeremiah, he may have been 'a eunuch for the Kingdom' to prophesy the fruitlessness of God's covenant with Zion. But Jesus lived in a society that was socially homosexual – with men finding spiritual intimacy with men, women with women. Jesus focused his social energies on forming a fraternity. And – although it is somewhat anachronistic to put it this way – for all we know, he was gay!

Read with a cool eye, the Bible stories positively discredit the idea that Jesus' family life was conventionally happy. What, then, made it *holy?*

The obvious answer is that *what makes a family holy is the presence of God.* The gospels do not tell JMJ stories to draw a fairytale portrait of utopic family bliss, but first and foremost to proclaim the Good News of God-with-us in our households, torn by whatever tragedy, disrupted by no-matter-what disaster, however unconventional they may be. Matthew and Luke make it clear, God adopted himself into an irregular branch of the human family, as an outward and visible sign of the Trinity's Divine determination to adopt us into their family, as a sacrament that God is really present in every household, for better and worse, for rich and for poor, in all our family systems, however healthy or dysfunctional, making them – like Bethlehem's stable, Nazareth's wood shop, and Calvary's hill – holy ground. The Good News of Christmas is, God-with-us does not abandon us, ever. And when we break down, when our families break apart for whatever reason, the blessed Trinity holds us each and all, wittingly or unwittingly, together in their family, with the unbreakable bands of their eternal love!

So far from idolising the conventional happy family, JMJ stories present Mary and Joseph as models of discipleship that subordinates natural human longing to the exigencies of Divine design. In Matthew and

Luke, Mary and Joseph plight their troth to a God whose plans stretch beyond anything they could ask or imagine. Like parents, prophets and artists in every age, they – yes, we – are called to open their hearts, to protect, nurture, make a home for creative possibilities beyond their understanding and permanently out of their control. Repeatedly, they risk their relationship and social security to allow something novel to happen. When Mary equivocates, does not understand the shepherds, the wise, Simeon's prophecy, or why Jesus is leaving her behind, her ears are open to hear the Divine Word of correction, her heart is ready to renew its assent: 'Be it unto me according to your Word!'

Emmanuel is the Good News of Christmas – God with us everywhere and always, in every household, single, gay-coupled, divorced, long-term heterosexually married, with or without 2.5 kids, a white picket fence and a dog! Like Mary and Joseph, we are called to writhe with labour pains, to sacrifice ourselves to birth and nurture blessing, by the tedium and anxiety of daily co-operation to open our hearts, to light up our homes to show forth God's love to an estranged and broken world!

[Preached at Christ Church, New Haven,
Christmas II, 2000]

SEVENTEEN

Gay Pride,
Humbled Church

For freedom Christ has set us free. Stand firm, therefore, and do not submit again to a yoke of slavery . . .

For you were called to freedom, brothers and sisters; only do not use your freedom as an opportunity for self-indulgence, but through love become slaves to one another. For the whole law is summed up in a single commandment, 'You shall love your neighbour as yourself.' If, however, you bite and devour one another, take care that you are not consumed by one another.

Live by the Spirit, I say, and do not gratify the desires of the flesh. For what the flesh desires is opposed to the Spirit, and what the Spirit desires is opposed to the flesh; for these are opposed to each other, to prevent you from doing what you want. But if you are led by the Spirit, you are not subject to the law. Now the works of the flesh are obvious: fornication, impurity, licentiousness, idolatry, sorcery, enmities, strife, jealousy, anger, quarrels, dissen-

sions, factions, envy, drunkenness, carousing, and things like these. I am warning you, as I warned you before: those who do such things will not inherit the kingdom of God.

By contrast, the fruit of the Spirit is love, joy, peace, patience, kindness, generosity, faithfulness, gentleness and self-control. There is no law against such things. And those who belong to Christ Jesus have crucified the flesh with its passions and desires. If we live by the Spirit, let us also be guided by the Spirit. (Galatians 5:1, 13–25)

Today is Gay Pride Sunday, and many of our gay and lesbian members and friends are participating in special parades and celebrations. As the label suggests, the accent is on the positive: to give up apologising for homosexual orientation and lifestyle, instead to affirm it as good, what we Christians would style a special giftedness, a calling from God.

Sadly, many Christians still disagree with this assessment. Some insist that homosexual activity is contrary to biblical norms. Ironically, one of their proof-texts is included in today's epistle lesson, where St Paul lists *porneia* – fornication, impurity and licentiousness – among the works of the flesh that separate one from God. Other passages include the 'Holiness Code' in Leviticus, which counts male homosexual acts among the 'abominations', and the first chapter of Romans where St Paul makes homosexual encounters paradigms of the depravity to which God abandons sinners. To the authority of the book, many would add church pronouncements and canon law, which recognise celibacy and heterosexual monogamy as the only legitimate options. These Christian brothers and sisters ask how we who celebrate Gay Pride Sunday can conscientiously contradict such prominent elements of our tradition.

Theirs is a fair question. In a nutshell, my answer is that both Church and Bible are human as well as Divine. Inevitably, Divine–human communication is filtered through culture, which highlights some things and screens others out. The Bible stories themselves range over a 2000-year period, during which social organisation, religious practice, norms and taboos vary considerably. Appeals to the Bible for ethical guidance make assumptions about how it is to be interpreted, give some passages or themes precedence over others. Such presuppositions are usually controversial, consciously or unconsciously driven by other concerns. This is why Christians can, in good faith, so radically disagree.

It is also why the contemporary relevance of biblical norms is often unclear. Sometimes, as in 1 Timothy 1:10, the reference is obscure: is St Paul talking about homosexual acts between consenting adults, or merely pagan temple prostitution? For other passages, meaning is straightforward, but applicability is in doubt. Early Mormons found precedent for polygamy in the patriarchs and Israelite kings, while appalled mainline Christians made them give it up as a condition of Utah's statehood. Few Christians feel generally bound by the Levitical code: e.g., we feel no qualms about wearing mixed-fibre clothes, we don't break the bowl just because a bug lands in the soup. Our Lord's only explicit remarks about sexual mores forbid divorce and remarriage. Yet, several decades ago, our Episcopal Church conceded that permission in this area is a present pastoral necessity. Despite his Damascus Road conversion, St Paul did not achieve full escape-velocity from his culture. His relationship to Christ gave him courage to trample Jewish taboos against eating with Gentiles. But in my opinion, 'God wasn't finished with him yet.' I don't believe he saw clearly in the area of sexuality or gender stereotypes. You haven't caught me obeying his injunction that women should keep silent in the church. And he probably knew even less about homosexual love than he did about the opposite sex!

Likewise, the Church's remarkable narrowness on this subject has a social-psychological explanation. For sexuality is one of the most powerful forces in human personality. Because lack of channelling produces ruin of great personal and collective proportions, social groups over-protect with rigid taboos and prohibitions, institutionalise repression, and forfeit creativity. Again, sexual identity and orientation are at once *central* to our self-images and *fragile*. Many feel safer in a society that narrows down the options, forces everyone into simple moulds. Deviation threatens by reminding the fearful that they don't really fit either! The Church, qua human institution seeking to maintain organisational control on chaotic seas, deploys merely human methods, and in doing so betrays the Gospel. For the survival of the Church is entrusted to the Holy Spirit, who is both omnipotent and infinitely creative and needs no help from taboos!

Personally, I take my clue to a Christian understanding of Gay Pride from the book of Acts, which relates how the Church handled its first major crisis. Recall how Christianity began as a sect of Judaism. When religious leaders first harassed, then instigated a government pogrom, fleeing Christians spread the Gospel to Diaspora Jews. They had no intention of addressing Gentiles. But when eavesdropping Gentiles heard and believed, the Holy Spirit unmistakably fell upon them, worked signs and wonders through them. When the apostles investigated, confirmed how the Spirit of God dared to violate Jewish taboos, the Jerusalem council weighed experience against tradition, agreed with the Spirit to count Gentiles in.

I am convinced that homosexual lifestyle is one way of living out Christian commitment, for some a positive vocation, because as a priest I have witnessed the Holy Spirit clearly at work in the lives of gay and lesbian persons. The AIDS epidemic forces our attention on hundreds of icons of Christ's passion, of resurrection courage and creativity, of sacrificial love that will not let brother or sister, friend, lover or stranger die alone. I have been awestruck by the spiritual depth in those left behind. As a spiritual director, I have nudged ex-fundamentalist gay men to come out of the closet to God in their prayers, only to watch their stature in Christ sky-rocket, their gifts burst into flower.

Our gay and lesbian brothers and sisters deserve a celebration. We have promised to support them in their life in Christ. The Lord our God, that Lover of Lovers, will hold us accountable for our failures on Judgement Day! What, then, shall we do?

First, Gay Pride Sunday is a day for the Church to humble herself by apologising to gay and lesbian persons, to repent before God for her collusion in the way society has persecuted them through the ages. Gay Pride Sunday is a day for the Church to ask forgiveness from gay and lesbian persons for all of the ways she has cramped their style, crushed the image of Christ in them. It is a day to vow fruits of repentance, to commit ourselves to erase all traces of discrimination from our canon law!

Second, Gay Pride Sunday is a day for the Church to humble herself, to confess her failure to nurture gay and lesbian persons by publicly identifying, canonising role models, both sexually active and celibate. For centuries, Mother Church has aborted her responsibility to teach us all how to be lovers in the image of Christ. Taboos and authoritarian pronouncements declare that all is forbidden, invite the counter-thesis that all is allowed. With homo- as with heterosexuality, not all things are helpful. Having idled in inarticulate gears for centuries, Mother Church now has become a 'foolish virgin' with little light to shed. Gay Pride Sunday is a day for Mother Church to humble herself, to beg her gay and lesbian children to teach her which patterns of love best focus the image of Christ in them.

Third, Gay Pride Sunday is a day for the Church to advertise how gays and lesbians number among the spiritually most advanced. Baptism, our birthing into God's family, cuts us off from every human blood line, cancels our entitlement to identify ourselves in merely human social terms. The epistle to the Hebrews says we are to count ourselves strangers and exiles upon the earth, because our true citizenship is in heaven. Those who slide readily into pre-established social niches are easily entombed by them. By contrast, the mis-fitting of gays and lesbians can free them to learn who they are directly from the Creator. The process of coming out is a prototype spiritual journey, in which the person has to wrestle in the desert, like Christ did, to invent a unique integrity. Gay Pride is a day for Mother Church to humble herself, to beg her gay and lesbian children to guide others on their way to God.

Fourth, Gay Pride Sunday is a day for the Church to humble herself, to seek to know from her gay and lesbian children what they have learned about God's own nature. Two weeks ago we celebrated the blessed Trinity, confessed the mystery that God in God's own essential nature is a society of persons eternally in love. Traditionally, the linguistic image – of Father, Son and Holy Spirit, all referred to as 'he' – is of same-gender love affairs. Even if we switch genders, the analogy is not to heterosexual monogamy. Who better than gay and lesbian Christians to give fresh insight into what trinitarian romance is like?

All in all, Gay Pride Sunday is a day of gospel re-versals: a day for old Mother Church to come out of the closet and confess her failures, to receive absolution from her priestly children, to parade with them behind Christ our Drum Major, onward to Zion, that beautiful City of God!

[Preached at St Augustine's-by-the-Sea,
Gay Pride Sunday, 1992]

EIGHTEEN

'Coming Out' in the Power of the Spirit

'Coming out' is a human assignment. God our Mother conceives each of us from eternity, inwardly forms, moulds limbs and arms, face and nose into something new, yet with family resemblance. God our Creator builds in gifts and strengths and vulnerabilities, breathes in Holy Spirit to make us partners in creation, first and foremost of ourselves. God holds us in the womb of her nurture, eagerly anticipates what we will make of all that potential, from what angle reflect, what treasured image and likeness bring out of the storehouse within.

'Coming out' is a process with its times, seasons and rhythms. Alternately, we need cosy caves for hibernation, to grow ourselves in ways so rich and yet so delicate, to gestate for a while freed from outside pressures and challenges. By turns, safe wombs become cramping and confining. Kicking and bumping against their

walls, we brave the birth canal. Empowered by the Spirit of new-formed integration, we burst forth into the wider world to test our vision, try our strength, to share Good News, to beautify and to heal. Eventually, having spent the energy of that experiment, we find ourselves pregnant again, retire with Mary to the hill country, prepare to give birth to more.

'Coming out' has many dimensions. We humans are complex characters: body as well as mind and spirit, unconscious as well as conscious selves. Beginning with body, we learn as infants to focus our vision, to touch finger to opposable thumb, to babble, crawl, eventually walk and leap and run. Leaving home for school, we come out intellectually, learn to read and write, venture new ideas, discover, reveal ourselves as persons with distinctive sympathies. Spiritually, too, we reach out from and beyond our experience, longing to embrace the One for whom we were made.

Coming out sexually, as sexual persons, can be the most difficult precisely because it is so important. For sexual identity lies at the heart of our very selves. Sexual energy is the sacrament of that creativity we bear in God's image. Yet, power and danger go together. No wonder society tries to harness *everybody's* sexual energy, pull everyone back with the tight reins of taboos. Pre-established cubby holes of heterosexual monogamy and celibacy are imposed to discourage anyone – even those who are heterosexual or have a genuine vocation to celibacy – from 'coming out' sexually. The tone is, 'Don't think about it, don't talk about it, perish the thought of praying about it! Just conform, or be cast into outer darkness where there is weeping and gnashing of teeth!' Marriage and monastery become their own kinds of closets.

What is wrong is not the thought that creativity needs structure; certainly it does if we are to dazzle as images of God. Rather the sin lies in enforcing wilfully mindless oversimplifications with cruelty, with habits of cover-up that darken everyone's mirror.

'Coming out' requires discernment. Even in Eden, we would face decisions. Our possibilities under-determine our identities because God made us to be creative like him. Developmental creatures by nature, even in utopia, we would find it confusing trying to figure out who we want to be.

Where family models lead astray, where Church and society shout 'don't tell', chop away at us left hands, try to blind eyes to fresh visions, the problems of what to say or do or be, before whom, where and when, multiply, threaten to crush. We walk a tightrope *between* fleeing with Joseph to Egypt to guard and nourish the gift that is in us; *and* striding out in the power of the Spirit to proclaim the Good News, that by the grace of God we are what we are; as members of Christ's Body, we are lesbian, bisexual, straight or gay.

Happily, *'coming out' has many contexts.* The media make it a matter of public announcement, with cameras and mikes and newspapers the next day. Repeatedly, seminarians and clergy face the problem, how open dare I be with the Church? The family? Old friends who never knew?

To 'beg' these questions for others is spiritual violence. Nor can we answer them for ourselves without retreating to the heart's secret closet, where we 'come out' to ourselves and to God. This spiritual exercise is fully reasonable. For more than anyone else, God is *for us*. Unlike merely human parents, God is not stuck with what he gets. God is our Creator: if God hadn't loved redheads, gays and lesbians, butch and drag, God could have made someone else! The Spirit of God is fully trustworthy, has no hidden agenda but the possibilities planted within us. The Spirit of God is wise and incredibly imaginative, a person of long and varied experience. She is never over-booked, ever available for spiritual companionship.

'Coming out' to God will give us courage for bold adventures. The more we come out from behind our fig leaf, not just know that God knows like 'Big Brother Watching You', but deliberately bare ourselves in the presence of our Divine Lover, the more we enjoy the strength of God's presence, come to see and delight in ourselves through God's eyes; the more we *experience* the vastness of Divine Love, its capacity to swallow up our self-doubts, fears of alien reprisals.

And so, whatever else this celebration may mean for you this evening, its deepest challenge is the same for all Christians: in your heart of hearts, commit yourself; in some new way, 'come out' to God!

[Preached at Marquand Chapel, Yale Divinity School, Coming Out Day, 1993]